THE ANSWER TO ANXIETY

THE ANSWER TO ANXIETY

How to Break Free from the Tyranny of Anxious Thoughts and Worry

JOYCE MEYER

NEW YORK • NASHVILLE

I would like to thank Beth Clark for her excellent editorial work on this book.

Copyright © 2023 by Joyce Meyer

Cover copyright © 2023 by Hachette Book Group, Inc.

Hachette Book Group supports the right to free expression and the value of copyright. The purpose of copyright is to encourage writers and artists to produce the creative works that enrich our culture.

The scanning, uploading, and distribution of this book without permission is a theft of the author's intellectual property. If you would like permission to use material from the book (other than for review purposes), please contact permissions@hbgusa.com. Thank you for your support of the author's rights.

FaithWords
Hachette Book Group
1290 Avenue of the Americas, New York, NY 10104
faithwords.com
twitter.com/faithwords

First Edition: February 2023

FaithWords is a division of Hachette Book Group, Inc. The FaithWords name and logo are trademarks of Hachette Book Group, Inc.

The publisher is not responsible for websites (or their content) that are not owned by the publisher.

The Hachette Speakers Bureau provides a wide range of authors for speaking events. To find out more, go to www.hachettespeakersbureau.com or call (866) 376-6591.

Library of Congress Cataloging-in-Publication Data has been applied for.

ISBNs: 978-1-5460-2917-5 (hardcover), 978-1-5460-0304-5 (large print), 978-1-5460-2918-2 (ebook)

Printed in the United States of America

LSC-C

Printing 1, 2022

CONTENTS

Anxiety and worry are common human responses to stressful situations. We all feel anxious, worried, or concerned at times. But if anxiety becomes severe enough, it may require medical attention, which could include some type of professional counseling and/or medication. Situations that typically require such intervention include long-term stress or unbalanced hormones or neurotransmitters. When therapy or medication is warranted, we should not feel ashamed of getting the help we need.

According to the Anxiety and Depression Association of America, "Anxiety disorders are the most common and pervasive mental disorders in the United States."[1] Take a look at these statistics[2]:

> "Anxiety disorders are the most common and pervasive mental disorders in the United States."

- Anxiety disorders affect 40 million adults in the United States (18.1 percent of the population) every year. Anxiety disorders are the most common mental illnesses in the United States.
- Only 36.9 percent of those suffering from anxiety receive treatment, even though it is highly treatable.

- Risk factors including genetics, brain chemistry, personality, and life events contribute to the development of anxiety disorders.
- Anxiety disorders and depression are linked. Almost half of people diagnosed with depression are also diagnosed with an anxiety disorder.
- Women are twice as likely to be affected by generalized anxiety disorder as men.
- Stress and anxiety affect everyone at one time or another.
- Stress is a response to a threat in a certain situation. Anxiety is a reaction to that stress.
- Anxiety disorders affect 25.1 percent of teenagers. Teens with untreated anxiety disorders are at higher risk for poor school performance, missing out on important social experiences, and substance abuse.
- Older adults experience anxiety at rates similar to teenagers, although anxiety disorders in this population are frequently associated with traumatic events such as a fall or acute illness.

Anxiety is a clinical term. As you can see, much research has been conducted regarding anxiety, and it is a serious problem. However, there is another type of anxiety that comes with our day-to-day trials and stressful situations. It is called worry.

> "Worrying is carrying tomorrow's load with today's strength."

Corrie Ten Boom said, "Worrying is carrying tomorrow's load with today's strength—carrying two days at once. It is moving into tomorrow ahead of time."[3] I think one reason people end up with serious anxiety or depression disorders is that they don't address the anxiety we all face daily and let it build until it becomes unhealthy or unmanageable. There are, of course, other more serious underlying causes of anxiety, such as abuse during childhood, severe long-lasting illness, loss of a loved one, working too hard for too long, not getting enough rest or sleep, and other conditions.

In this book, I want to address the daily anxieties and worries that we deal with simply because we live in a sinful world that presents us with frequent problems. Jesus says that we will have trouble while we are in the world, but to take heart, or cheer up, because He has overcome the world (John 16:33). If we can learn to deal with daily anxieties quickly, they will have no opportunity to turn into mental disorders. We can and should learn from God's Word how to deal with our daily situations.

If you deal with daily anxieties quickly, they have no opportunity to turn into mental disorders.

The quicker we refuse to worry when we are tempted to do so, the less likely we are to have serious problems with anxiety.

My husband, Dave, never worries. Part of the reason for this is his natural temperament and part of it is his trust in God. He truly believes God will take care of him, and he has a genuine revelation of 1 Peter 5:7, which says to cast "the whole of your care [all your anxieties, all your

worries, all your concerns, once and for all] on Him, for
He cares for you affectionately and cares about you watchfully" (AMPC). I have a son-in-law and a daughter-in-law
who are the same way. They are genuinely at peace, no
matter what is happening in their life.

However, I've learned that although some people seem
calm no matter what the situation may be, they may inter-
nalize their frustration, fear, and worry. This can be more
harmful than expressing their negative emotions. I've
heard that people either explode or implode if they don't
learn to deal with their emotions properly. For years, I was
the type to explode, but eventually all of my explosions
also caused me to implode. In December 2017, after years
of unreasonable stress caused by many situations, I fell
apart, so to speak, and became extremely ill due to a condition that had taken years to develop and took more than
eighteen months to recover from.

The illness turned out to be a blessing in disguise. It
was a turning point in my life, and it provoked me to
make changes I had needed to make for a long, long time.

> *Excessive stress left unaddressed will lead to a crisis of some kind.*

If excessive stress is left unad-
dressed, it will build to the point
where our bodies, minds, and
emotions simply can't deal with
it any longer, and we will reach a
crisis point of some kind. Sooner or later we must admit,
"I just cannot do it all anymore."

Trusting God to take care of the things we cannot do
anything about and trusting Him to give us the direction

we need to handle what we can do ourselves should be our normal response to problems. When we try to solve our problems through worry and reasoning (trying to figure out in our minds why something has happened or what to do about it), we don't get answers, but we do get frustration and more stress.

People don't want to worry when they have problems, but most people would say that they can't prevent themselves from doing it. This, of course, is not true, because Jesus tells us not to worry (Matthew 6:25). There must be a way for us not to worry, because Jesus never tells us to do something that is impossible.

I believe the Bible gives us an easy and understandable formula regarding how to stay in peace instead of being anxious when we have problems that create stress. It's Philippians 4:6–7 (NKJV):

> Be anxious for nothing, but in everything by prayer and supplication, with thanksgiving, let your requests be made known to God; and the peace of God, which surpasses all understanding, will guard your hearts and minds through Christ Jesus.

These two verses offer the formula on which this book is based, which you'll discover as you keep reading. It's simple, as many of God's answers to our problems are, but we tend to complicate things that could be simple by doing things our way instead of His way.

Charles Stanley says, "We could all work up a nervous breakdown in thirty seconds if we really wanted to."[4] I would say that on most days, we can find something to worry about unless we choose not to, and I have learned that every day I spend worrying is a day I waste and one I will never get back. I am not interested in wasting any more of my time doing things that do not work and tend to make me miserable.

Every day you spend worrying is a day you waste and one you will never get back.

In order not to worry and be anxious, we must learn new ways—God's ways—to handle our problems and challenges. I am happy to be writing this book because I plan to get help from it as I study to write it. At this very moment, I have two different situations in my life that I don't want to worry about, and I am asking God to help me. Worry keeps coming to my mind, and I keep refusing it. But worry is a very persistent enemy. In order to live life without worry and anxiety, we must be just as persistent at resisting it as our enemy the devil is at pressuring us with it.

God's will for us is peace, not worry and anxiety, so I pray you will join me as we learn together how to live a worry- and anxiety-free life.

THE ANSWER TO ANXIETY

CHAPTER 1

Be Anxious for Nothing

Worry a little bit every day and in a lifetime you will lose a couple of years. If something is wrong, fix it if you can. But train yourself not to worry. Worry never fixes anything.

Mary Hemingway[5]

God allots each of us a certain amount of time to live on earth, and we either waste it or use it wisely. When that time is gone, we can never get it back, so it seems that we would not want to waste even one minute, but we do. Sometimes we waste our time by doing frivolous or foolish things that bear no fruit. Often, though, we waste our time feeling sorry for ourselves, being angry or depressed, letting fear control us, feeling anxious or worried, or allowing ourselves to express other negative emotions. I hope this book will help you not to waste any more of your valuable time being anxious or worried about anything.

When we spend today being anxious or worried about tomorrow, we waste today and accomplish nothing that will change tomorrow. Jesus teaches us to live one day at a time and not to spend any of them worrying:

> *When we waste today being anxious, we accomplish nothing that will change tomorrow.*

Therefore I tell you, do not worry about your life, what you will eat or drink; or about your body, what you will wear. Is not life more than food, and the body more than clothes? Look at the birds of the air; they do not sow or reap or store away in barns, and yet your heavenly Father feeds them. Are you not much more valuable than they? Can any one of you by worrying add a single hour to your life? And why do you worry about clothes? See how the flowers of the field grow. They do not labor or spin. Yet I tell you that not even Solomon in all his splendor was dressed like one of these. If that is how God clothes the grass of the field, which is here today and tomorrow is thrown into the fire, will he not much more clothe you—you of little faith? So do not worry, saying, "What shall we eat?" or "What shall we drink?" or "What shall we wear?" For the pagans run after all these things, and your heavenly Father knows that you need them. But seek first his kingdom and his righteousness, and all these things will be given to you as well. Therefore do not worry about tomorrow, for tomorrow will worry about itself. Each day has enough trouble of its own.

Matthew 6:25–34

Let's think about what this Scripture passage teaches. First, Jesus says not to worry about anything—food, drink, or clothing (v. 25). For that matter, don't worry about anything in your life, because your life is more important to God than all the "things" you want and need.

Second, we should do a little bird watching. This may sound funny, but it is exactly what Jesus suggests we do. Birds are everywhere, so we should not have a hard time watching them. Birds are not nervous, anxious, or worried. They fly around happily waiting for their next meal to appear. The meal may consist of seeds that have fallen from a plant or tree, bird seed that someone has put out because they have a bird feeder, a worm, or some kind of bug on the ground, which God provides for them. Verse 26 tells us that God provides for the birds and says that we are more valuable than they are, so why should we doubt that He will provide for us?

Then comes the question we should all ask ourselves in verse 27: Does worry do any good, and can it add even a single hour to our life? It cannot add to our life, but it can steal from it.

Jesus then asks why we worry about our clothing (v. 28). Maybe you don't worry about clothes, but there is likely something pertaining to everyday life that you do worry about. Jesus challenges us to look at the flowers and notice how He clothes them so beautifully. They never labor or spin, and they don't worry or become fearful and anxious. But not even King Solomon, in all his glory and splendor, was dressed as fine as a little flower (vv. 28–29). Take some time and look at your flowers. If you don't have any, go to a park or a garden and just look at how beautiful and amazingly different each one is.

Jesus also mentions something we usually don't think about: the grass. He takes care of grass, which is here today and gone tomorrow (v. 30).

Don't be a person of little faith. Have big faith, because God knows what you need. Unbelievers seek and worry about necessities such as food, drink, and clothing. But, as believers, you

Have big faith, because God knows what you need.

and I are to "seek first his kingdom and his righteousness, and all these things will be given to you as well" (v. 33).

Jesus continues, saying, "Therefore do not worry about tomorrow, for tomorrow will worry about itself. Each day has enough trouble of its own" (v. 34). To that, I say, "Amen!" In the past month, Dave and I had to have our television repaired. We also had a larger gas line put in our home because our generator wasn't working correctly, and after paying several hundred dollars for it, the generator still doesn't work as it should. And every time we have a really hard rain and the wind blows in a certain direction, we get water in our house. This has gone on for almost two years, and no one can figure out why it happens. In addition, Dave's golf cart needed a new battery. I found out I need cataract surgery. What concerns me most is that my eyes are already terribly dry, and cataract surgery makes them drier, at least for a few months. The surgery will require two procedures, one on each eye. In the midst of the two operations, I need to try to do as much teaching for television in the studio as I possibly can, so I don't get too far behind with our daily program. I also have a speaking engagement and have no idea what my eyes will feel like or how well I will be able to see.

I share this glimpse into my life because I want you to know that challenges happen to everyone. It is part of life, and each situation eventually gets solved. Worrying about it doesn't change a thing, except that it steals our peace and joy.

Jesus is telling us in Matthew 6:25–34 to take life one day at a time—and not to worry about anything—because each day has all we can handle. Natural storms

> *Like natural storms, the personal storms that come into our lives are often unexpected.*

are not always in the weather forecast, and often the storms that come into our lives are also unexpected. However, people of great faith are ready for anything.

Paul teaches in Philippians 4:13 that we "can do all things through Christ," who strengthens us (NKJV). The amplification of this verse says that we are "ready for anything and equal to anything through Him" that comes our way (AMPC). This is a great promise to meditate on regularly. It builds our faith and prepares us for whatever a day may bring.

In addition to keeping Philippians 4:13 in mind, we should have the same attitude that the missionary Hudson Taylor had:

> I am no longer anxious about anything, as I realise this; for He, I know, is able to carry out *His will*, and His will is mine. It makes no matter where He places me, or how. That is rather for Him to consider than for me; for in the easiest positions He must give me His grace, and in the most difficult His grace is sufficient.[6]

What Are Anxiety and Worry?

I'm sure you know what I mean when I use the words *anxiety* and *worry* because everyone has experience with these feelings. I have explained them briefly, but let's think more thoroughly about what they mean. The simplest way

I know to define anxiety is to say that it means spending today trying to figure out tomorrow or spending today fearing or dreading tomorrow. It is an uneasy

Anxiety is spending today dreading tomorrow.

feeling of worry, uncertainty, dread, fear, or agitation. In the Bible, anxiety is depicted as the common human reaction to stressful situations.

Stressful situations abound in many of our lives. I believe most of us always have something we could worry about unless we intentionally choose not to. The psalmist confessed that when anxiety was great within him, God's comfort calmed him down and brought him joy (Psalm 94:19), and Saul's father was anxious during a time when his donkeys were lost (1 Samuel 9:5), so we can see that people throughout history have had to deal with anxiety and worry.

Anxiety, if not confronted, can lead to more serious problems—depression, for example. Proverbs 12:25 says that anxiety can cause depression: "Anxiety in the heart of man causes depression, but a good word makes it glad" (NKJV). Anxiety is inconsistent with trusting God, which is what we are to do at all times and in every situation. But

anxiety has always been an unusually difficult challenge
for us, and it always will be. It is Satan's method of stealing
the peace that Jesus died to give
us. Every time a situation arises

> *Every time a situation causes us to be anxious, we must renew our trust in God instead of being anxious.*

that could be stressful or would
cause us to be anxious or worried, we have to renew our commitment to trust God instead of
being anxious.

Anxiety is rooted in fear. For example, we become anxious when we are afraid we will lose something or someone important to us, when we are afraid we won't be taken
care of, when we are afraid that something bad will happen to us, or when we are afraid we won't get what we want
or need. Because we are afraid, we try to take care of situations ourselves. This, of course, causes us to worry and
reason as we try to come up with solutions. We cannot
enjoy peace of mind if our minds are filled with thoughts
of how we can solve our problems.

> A man's mind plans his way [as he journeys
> through life], but the Lord directs his steps and
> establishes them.
>
> Proverbs 16:9 AMP

I am thankful that even though we make our plans, if
they are not right, God does interrupt them and direct
our steps in the right direction. His thoughts and ways are
higher than our thoughts and ways (Isaiah 55:8–9).

When we worry, we allow our thoughts to rotate around and around the same situation, playing out the potential outcomes in our mind. Most of the terrible outcomes we imagine don't happen, but the fear that they might happen causes us to be tormented.

Approximately five hundred years ago, Michel de Montaigne said: "My life has been filled with terrible misfortune; most of which never happened."[7] Those events happened only in his mind and imagination, but he suffered as though they actually took place.

> Most of what people worry will happen never happens.

Don Joseph Goewey, author of *The End of Stress*, says that about 85 percent of what people worry will happen never happens.[8]

The Bible tells us to meditate on God's Word (Joshua 1:8), and I tell people that if they know how to worry, they know how to meditate. We can meditate on God's promises to us, or we can meditate on our problems; the choice is ours. One produces bad fruit, and one produces good fruit. One steals our joy and may even damage our health, while the other gives us peace and enables us to enjoy our life while God is working on our problems.

Philippians 4:6–7 (NKJV), the scriptures on which this book is based, is one of my favorite Bible passages:

> Be anxious for nothing, but in everything by prayer and supplication, with thanksgiving, let your requests be made known to God; and the

peace of God, which surpasses all understanding, will guard your hearts and minds through Christ Jesus.

As I mentioned in the introduction to this book, I see in these verses four distinct ways we can respond when we encounter problems; they are actions that will allow us to enjoy life no matter what happens:

1. We are not to be anxious.
2. We are to pray.
3. We are to be thankful.
4. We are to enjoy peace.

I truly believe that if we can understand the power of Philippians 4:6–7, we will find the answer to anxiety. This is my go-to Scripture passage any time I begin to worry. I have memorized these verses, so I rehearse them in my mind, and sometimes I even open my Bible and look at them.

Any time I have a problem, my first instinct is to worry, but after doing that for a few minutes, I remind myself that I have often traveled the road of worry, and it has never once taken me to my desired destination, which is

> *The road of worry has never taken me to my desired destination.*

peace. It has never given me a solution to the problems I face. Worrying is like rocking in a rocking chair all day: It keeps you busy but gets you nowhere.

The formula for dealing with our problems begins with "Be anxious for nothing" (Philippians 4:6 NKJV). This is easy to read and easy to say, but sometimes it's difficult to do. People often need some simple steps to help them not to be anxious about anything, and I have identified five keys to overcoming anxiety, which we will explore in the next several chapters.

CHAPTER 2

Five Keys to Overcoming Anxiety, Part 1

Anxiety does not empty to-morrow of its sorrows, but only empties to-day of its strength.

Charles Spurgeon[9]

People suggest all kinds of ways to overcome anxiety, from medication to relaxation techniques to taking a vacation at the beach. I'm sure many of these ways can be helpful on some level, but in this chapter and the next one, I'd like to share five specific keys that enable me to overcome anxiety in my life, and I believe they will empower you to overcome the anxiety you deal with at times too.

Key #1: Remember Past Victories

One very helpful way I deal with problems is to think about troubles I have faced in the past that God has resolved without my help. There are times when God shows us something to do about a situation, and if He does, we should do it. But if He doesn't show us anything, we should take a stand of faith in Him, trusting Him to do what we cannot do.

For a long time, I tried to change myself into the person I thought God wanted me to be, but all I got was frustrated. I was afraid that God was not pleased with me, and I felt guilty most of the time because I didn't measure up to what I thought the Bible told me I should be.

I finally gave up, told God I could not change myself, and invited Him to do it if He wanted to. I saw in 2 Corinthians 3:18 that if we contemplate (think about) God's glory, we are being transformed into Christ's image, from one degree of glory to the next, meaning from one measure of Christlikeness to another.

How do we change? Certainly not through worry or fear that God will reject us if we don't change, but by studying His Word and letting the power inherent in it transform us. We should pay close attention to the fact that He changes us "from glory to glory" (2 Corinthians 3:18 NKJV). This means the changes we need don't all come at once, but in degrees.

God has changed me into a different person than I was forty-five years ago when I first began to seriously study His Word, but the transformation certainly didn't happen all at once. He is still changing me, and I am delighted to let Him do so.

We can be conformed or we can be transformed. Romans 12:2 says: "Do not conform to the pattern of this world, but be transformed by the renewing of your mind." As we do this, we can enjoy the good plan that God has for us. As we learn to think as God thinks, we will eventually do what He wants us to do.

The Word of God renews our *The Word of God renews your mind.* mind. It teaches us how to think as God thinks and to think according to His will and plan for our lives. It is not His will for us to worry, fret, or be anxious and fearful every time we have a problem or face some kind of trouble. The world responds to problems and difficulties with worry and anxiety, but Jesus died to give us— His followers—a new way of living, and His goal for us is peace. The renewing of the mind takes time and determination. Most of us have spent a long time thinking as the world thinks, and this way of thinking won't be broken overnight. However, if you begin to do the right thing over and over, it will eventually leave no room in your mind and life for negativity such as worry and anxiety.

God's Word is truth, and only the truth makes us free (John 8:32). Truth is more powerful than facts. The fact may be that

> God's Word is the truth that makes you free.

you have a serious problem that needs solving, but the truth is that you cannot solve it without God's help, so cast your care on Him and let Him take care of you.

When the psalmist struggled with worry and anxiety, he remembered past victories God had given him: "I will remember the deeds of the Lord; yes, I will remember your miracles of long ago" (Psalm 77:11).

Perhaps you don't have anyone to encourage you in your time of trouble. If not, you can encourage yourself in the Lord by meditating on His promises and remembering how faithful He has been to you in the past.

More than thirty years ago, I was diagnosed with breast cancer. I had gone to the doctor for my regular check-up, which included a mammogram. To my great surprise, I received a call from my doctor saying they had found a small tumor that looked suspicious and that I needed to have a biopsy. I was a little worried, but not much, because I felt sure they would find the tissue benign.

That was not the case. The doctors concluded that I

had a very fast-growing type of cancer and that the best course of action at that time was to remove the breast. Talk about being surprised by trouble! I was in shock. This was one of those "not all storms are in the forecast" moments in my life.

At the time, our ministry was young and financially dependent on offerings given at a weekly meeting I held. After surgery, I would not be able to do those meetings for at least two weeks, and the doctor didn't recommend going back that soon. I confess that I was worried about the cancer, the type of treatment I might need after the operation, and what would happen to the ministry during my down time. I was afraid and anxious, and I worried continually.

Then one day, in the very early hours of the morning, I woke up and felt the familiar fear and worry. I cried out to God to help me, and He whispered in my heart that He would take care of me. This was a word from God for me, and I suddenly knew that everything would be all right. I didn't know how God would take care of me, but I knew He would.

He told me to stay positive and to make only positive comments, such as "God loves me." "All things work together for good to those who love God and are called according to His purpose," based on Romans 8:28. "God, I trust You!" And "God is good."

I had to wait about ten days before the surgery, and they were ten very challenging days. Fear and worry would come, and I would purposefully call to mind that God had promised to take care of me. I would then declare the positive statements based on Scripture that God had placed on my heart, and I could literally feel my emotions calming down as I spoke them.

During the surgery, the doctors were able to remove all of the tumor. As they normally do, they took some lymph nodes from under my arm and tested them to see if the cancer had spread. After waiting several more days, I heard the good news that it had not spread.

I was sent to an oncologist to see what further treatment I would need, and she said, "None. Your problem is solved!" More than three decades have passed since this experience, and each year, my mammogram always comes back clear of any problems. Just a few days ago, I had my test for this year, and once again the report said everything was normal. Thanks be to God!

After I had the surgery and while I was recovering at home, we were very thankful that I no longer had cancer, but we still needed money to cover the ministry expenses until I could get back to work. One night, we were sitting in our family room watching television and the doorbell rang. When Dave answered, a man we didn't know handed him a check for $10,000 and told him that God had directed him to give it to us. Victory! I still think of that great victory when I have a problem and am anxious and worried, and I know that God will be faithful again just as He was then.

Key #2: Fight the Good Fight of Faith

The apostle Paul encourages us in 1 Timothy 6:12, saying, "Fight the good fight of the faith. Take hold of the eternal life to which you were called when you made your good confession in the presence of many witnesses." To "fight the good fight of faith" means there will be times of trouble when we must stand our ground and continue trusting God even when it is difficult. Worry and anxiety bombard our minds, and we must keep up a relentless regimen of meditating on God's Word and remembering past victories.

Meditate on God's Word and remember past victories.

We may even need to talk to ourselves. I do this regularly. I might say something such as, "Joyce, you don't have to worry about this or try to figure it out. God is faithful, and He will give you the answer to your problem. Stand your ground and be firm in faith, because all things are possible with God."

When negative thoughts attack your mind, the attack will cease if you declare the promises of God. You cannot think two thoughts at once, so thinking on the good thing will push the negative thing out of your mind. You may have to repeat this process many times. Remember that the devil won't give up easily, but you can outlast him if you are determined to do so. As 1 Timothy 6:12 encourages, fight the good fight of faith like a good soldier in the army of the Lord.

You may wonder how long it will take for victory to

come. I cannot tell you that. Only God knows the right timing for your breakthrough. Galatians 6:9 teaches not to be weary in doing what is right because we will reap in due time if we do not give up. "When, God, when?" is a big question that we all want answered, but God rarely answers it. He wants us to trust Him, and to do that we must live with unanswered questions. We don't need to know all of the answers as long as we know the One who does know, and that is Jesus.

God knows what we need, and whether He seems early or late, He knows the exact right time to provide for us. If He seems to take a long time, He may be stretching or testing our faith. Believe it or not, this is good for all of us. If you go to the gym and begin lifting weights because you want more muscles, you cannot get them without your muscles getting a little sore. Muscles have to be worked in order to grow, and our faith is the same way.

Jesus spoke of little faith (Matthew 8:26; Luke 12:28) and great faith (Matthew 8:10; 15:28). I don't know about you, but I want great faith, and I know that I will never have it unless my little faith is forced to work so it becomes greater. The more God requires us to use our faith, the stronger it will become. A good thing to say when you are fighting the good fight of faith and it hurts is "I'm

> *The more God requires you to use your faith, the stronger it becomes.*

growing!" Doing what is right when it is easy doesn't help us grow to the next level, but doing right when it is difficult does.

The Bible says, "Without faith it is impossible to please Him, for he who comes to God must believe that He is, and that He is a rewarder of those who diligently seek Him" (Hebrews 11:6 NKJV). It is not our works that please God, but our faith in Him. He rewards those who diligently seek Him, and the key word here is *diligently*, which means without giving up, being steadfast, standing strong, and being determined to do the right thing no matter how long it takes.

As Christians, we do have work that must be done, but it should be Spirit-led, not works of the flesh. In other words, it should not consist of things we plan and plot because we think they will get us what we want. The Bible says, "Be still, and know that I am God" (Psalm 46:10). If we want to see God move in our lives and do things that amaze us, we must learn to be still, inside and out.

If you want to see God move in your life, learn to be still, inside and out.

When you are tempted to be anxious, don't worry. Instead, pray, give thanks, and let the peace that passes understanding keep your heart and mind in Christ. Let your mind rest from continually rotating around and around your problems, searching for answers. Use it to remember past victories and to fight the good fight of faith. Replace that bad habit with the good habit of letting your mind rotate around and around the promises of God.

CHAPTER 3

Five Keys to Overcoming Anxiety, Part 2

The beginning of anxiety is the end of faith, and the beginning of true faith is the end of anxiety.

George Müller[10]

I hope the first two keys to overcoming anxiety are already proving helpful to you. Let's continue our study of these keys so you will be better equipped to deal with the anxieties and worries you may be facing right now or will face in the future.

Key #3: Believe that God Is in Control

Let me remind you that God is always with you, and He is in control. You are never alone, because when you accepted Jesus as your Savior, He sent the Holy Spirit to live in you to help and strengthen you at all times, especially when you face trials and difficulties. It's so amazing to realize that through a personal relationship with God, you can talk to Him anytime, anywhere you are. And because prayer is such an important part of applying the keys to overcoming anxiety, I'm including several chapters about this subject later on in the book.

In addition, remember that many other people are going through situations similar to yours or circumstances that are much worse. No matter how bad a problem seems to be, people are dealing with things that are more difficult than what we are facing, and it's helpful to remember that.

No matter how bad your problems, there are people who are dealing with worse.

Feeling that we are the only one enduring difficulty can draw us into self-pity if we are not careful. When Elijah, the Old Testament prophet, was having a rough time because the wicked queen, Jezebel, had said she would kill him, he told God that he was the only prophet left in the land:

> He replied, "I have been very zealous for the Lord God Almighty. The Israelites have rejected your covenant, torn down your altars, and put your prophets to death with the sword. I am the only one left, and now they are trying to kill me too."
>
> 1 Kings 19:14

But God told Elijah in 1 Kings 19:18 that He had seven thousand people who had not bowed their knee to Baal. Elijah thought he was the only one, but he was wrong.

No matter what you may think, you are not the only person suffering, the only one waiting on God, or the only one struggling with worry and anxiety. I encourage you: While you are going through your difficulty, pray for others who are also suffering. This morning I received a text message from a woman who has cancer and is in tremendous pain. She told me she is praying for my cataract surgery. She could have been feeling sorry for herself because of her situation and thinking she was the only one suffering. But she was thinking of me, and I'm sure she was also thinking of others who are facing difficulties.

While you are suffering, pray for others who are also suffering.

The less we focus our minds on ourselves and our situations, the better off we will be. God promises that He will never leave us or forsake us (Joshua 1:5). This thought always comforts me, and I pray it comforts you too.

Sometimes we forget that God is with us at all times and that He is in control. But we should never despair. To despair means to be utterly without a way, to be quite at a loss and without resources, or to have no hope or to give up. I can assure you that no child of God ever needs to despair. Jesus is the way maker. He says, "I am the way" (John 14:6). He will make a way in the wilderness and provide rivers in the desert (Isaiah 43:19 ESV). I remember times when I could not see any way to solve a particular problem, but God made a way. One door may close, but if it does, God will open another one. Believe me when I say that God is never without an answer to any problem we have. All things are possible with Him (Matthew 19:26).

God is never without an answer to your problems.

Anxiety occurs when we spend today trying to get answers for tomorrow. It reminds me of when the Israelites tried to collect tomorrow's manna today (Exodus 16:16–20). This bread-like substance that God provided for their daily nourishment became rotten and began to stink if people hoarded it. Some individuals have what they might call "rotten, stinking lives" because they don't know how to live one day at a time, believing and trusting that God is in control.

I noted earlier that I find myself worrying about two

situations going on in my life right now. When I do, I have to remind myself of the same truths I am encouraging you to remember: I cannot do anything about these problems, but I do know that God can, and I know that He is in control. I may have to remind myself of this twenty times each day, but in my heart, I know it is true.

We often tell God what we can and cannot do. When we have problems, we assure Him we just cannot take any more, but He knows what we can endure. He will never allow more to come upon us than we can bear, and He will always provide a way out (1 Corinthians 10:13).

We don't have to have all the answers to all our problems, because God has them, and He is with us. At just the right time, He will reveal what we should do. Be assured that God is in control, that He is good, and that He loves you more than you could ever understand.

Key #4: Trust God

God wants us to trust Him completely. Trust is not worry, anxiety, reasoning, or fear. Trust produces rest, peace, hope, and a positive attitude. Trust shouts that you know and totally believe that God is in control.

Anxiety is a method by which we try to figure out what only God knows.

Worry and anxiety are methods by which we try to figure out what only God knows. If we trust Him, He will give us answers at the right time. But if we worry, all we end up with is a headache. Many times, God's answer is something we could not have even imagined.

"When, God, When?"

As you read in the previous chapter, one of our big questions when we are trusting God to do something is "When, God, when?" Even if we reach the place where we truly trust God, we at least want to know when He will give us the breakthrough we need. He will eventually do it, but it will be in His timing, not ours. He probably won't be early, but He promises that He won't be late.

Paul and Silas were in prison, and at midnight they were still singing and praising God (Acts 16:24–26). Other prisoners were listening. Paul and Silas were being good witnesses to the people around them. What kind of example do you set for others when you are in times of trials and trouble?

What kind of example do you set for others in your time of trials and trouble?

As Paul and Silas sang and praised God, God suddenly opened the doors to the prison, and they were released. Don't despair; your *suddenly* may be on the way.

Sometimes God delivers us from a situation quickly, and at other times we have to go through it for a season. If God decides you must go through something, then set your mind to go through it, because in that circumstance, the only way out is through. But remember that you are never alone. David writes, "Yea, though I walk through the valley of the shadow of death, I will fear no evil" (Psalm 23:4 NKJV). He had to go through the pain and the difficulty, just as we often do. He said he would fear no evil, but this does not mean he didn't feel fear trying to defeat him. The truth is that we can feel fear and still trust God. David also writes, "Whenever I am afraid, I will trust in You" (Psalm 56:3 NKJV).

Whenever you feel fear, you can still trust in God.

Your flesh may feel one thing, yet your heart can know the truth of God's Word. David knew that God was in control; therefore, even if he felt fear, he still trusted God. In my reading, I came upon this story about fear that I'd like to share with you.

Control Your Fears, or Be Controlled by Them

An old legend tells of a mouse who was afraid of cats. She wished she could become a cat so that she no longer had to be afraid of cats. Her wish came true, and she turned into a cat. Then she saw a dog and was afraid again. She wished she could become a dog. Her wish was granted, and she turned into a dog. Then she saw a lion and was afraid again. She wished she could become a lion. Her wish was granted, and she turned into a lion. Then she saw a man with a gun taking aim at her and was afraid again. She wished she could become a human. Her wish was granted, and she turned into a human. But one day, when she was sitting in her house, she saw a mouse and was terrified of the mouse!

We cannot escape the cycle of fear any other way than by casting our cares upon Jesus.

"Why God, Why?"

The question "Why, God, why?" torments us when we find ourselves in situations that we don't understand and that require our trust in God. When we encounter trouble, we often ask God, "Why is this happening to me?" Trials come our way for many reasons. Sometimes our faith is simply being tested. Sometimes we have opened a door for the devil to work in our lives through unforgiveness or disobedience of some kind. Sometimes troubles come because we are studying God's Word and growing spiritually, and Satan tries to stop our progress by distracting us with problems. Sometimes the worries of life and other things crowd out the Word we have heard (Mark 4:15–19). Sometimes problems arise simply because we live in a world full of troubles.

When I face difficulties, I find it is best to ask God if I have opened a door for the enemy in some way. If He shows me that I have, then I work with Him to close it tightly, asking Him to help me through the Holy Spirit and to strengthen me in that particular weakness. If God doesn't show me anything I have done to invite the enemy into my life to stir up trouble, then I know it is an attack of the devil and that God will intervene at just the right time. Let me say again: *God is in control!* There are only two times the devil will attack you—when

> *The devil will attack you when you have done something wrong and when you have done something right.*

you have done something wrong and when you have done something right. Continue loving God and trusting Him to help you regardless of why Satan is coming against you.

> But thanks be to God, who in Christ always leads us in triumphal procession, and through us spreads the fragrance of the knowledge of him everywhere.
>
> 2 Corinthians 2:14 ESV

Notice in this verse that God *always* leads us into triumph, and maintaining a thankful heart—an attitude of gratitude—is a vital part of trusting Him, especially while we're waiting for our breakthrough to come. In fact, being thankful is so important that I want to focus on it later on in a few chapters.

We read in John 14:27 that Jesus has given us His peace. He goes on to say, "Do not let your hearts be troubled, neither let them be afraid. [Stop allowing yourselves to be agitated and disturbed; and do not permit yourselves to be fearful and intimidated and cowardly and unsettled]" (AMPC). So, even though Jesus has given us peace, we still need to stop allowing ourselves to do things that lead to anxiety.

You may be thinking, *Joyce, this is exactly what I want to do, but I don't know how.* There are several keys to this, and

I don't want you to miss any of them, so let me remind you of the ones already mentioned in this book:

1. Remember past victories.
2. Fight the good fight of faith.
3. Believe that God is in control.
4. Trust God.

Key #5: Choose to Believe How Much God Loves You

Remember that worry and anxiety are rooted in the fear that we won't be taken care of or that something bad will happen to us, as I mentioned in chapter 1. The assurance that you will be taken care of and that God will protect you is found in 1 John 4:18: "Perfect love casts out fear" (NKJV). Perfect love is the love that God has for His children, and that includes you. Please read this verse in the Amplified Bible, Classic Edition:

> There is no fear in love [dread does not exist], but full-grown (complete, perfect) love turns fear out of doors and expels every trace of terror! For fear brings with it the thought of punishment, and [so] he who is afraid has not reached the full maturity of love [is not yet grown into love's complete perfection].

This scripture teaches us that if we are still afraid of not being taken care of, we need to grow in the knowledge that God loves us unconditionally, perfectly, and everlastingly. This knowledge usually takes time to develop, because we have difficulty believing that God could or would love us, due to our imperfections. Actually, it is *because* of our imperfections that God sent Jesus to die for us and take the punishment we deserved because of our sin.

> It is because of your imperfections that God sent Jesus to die for you and take the punishment you deserve.

I had to spend several years studying God's love for me in order to get my mind completely renewed in this area. Because of the sexual abuse I experienced from my father and being abandoned by my mother, I was convinced that if I didn't take care of myself, nobody else would take care of me. My parents certainly would not take care of me, nor would any of the other people I asked for help. However, God is not like people, and we cannot judge how He will treat us according to how others have treated us.

Let me encourage you to pray and ask God to help you grow in the revelation of how much He loves you. He loves all of us perfectly, and therefore we don't have to worry or be anxious when we have problems.

CHAPTER 4

The Miracle of Prayer

Therefore I tell you, whatever you ask for in prayer, believe that you have received it, and it will be yours.

Mark 11:24

Prayer is one of the greatest privileges we have, and I believe it is essential to overcoming anxiety. As I've grown in my relationship with Jesus throughout the years, I've come to the place where it continually amazes me. I can remember when I used to say, "Well, I guess there's nothing left for me to do but pray." I hear some people say this today, but this way of thinking is totally misguided. Prayer should never be the last thing we do after we have done everything else we can think of; it should be our first response in every situation. Pastor Rick Warren says, "The more you pray, the less you'll panic. The more you worship, the less you worry. You'll feel more patient and less pressured."[11]

I try to remember to pray and ask God to solve my problems the minute they arise. After studying God's Word for forty-five years and going through many challenging situations, I have definitely learned that one prayer can accomplish more in a moment than I could accomplish in a lifetime.

> *A prayer can accomplish more in a moment than you can in a lifetime.*

Some people do not truly understand prayer. Prayer is not an obligation we are required to fulfill as Christians; it is the greatest privilege we have. Prayer can be simple yet powerful, unless we complicate it through a lack of understanding what it really is.

Prayer is simply talking to God, just as we would talk to a good friend. He is all-powerful and wants to help us in every difficulty we face. However, we have not because we ask not (James 4:2). Too often we fail to ask Him for what we need, and we suffer for a long time because we look to every other source we know of before looking to Him.

Learn to pray immediately when you are anxious or worried about anything. Don't wait. There is no reason to wait, because God is available to help you the moment you call upon Him.

Pray immediately when you become anxious.

Definite Requests

I love the Amplified Bible, Classic Edition's rendering of Philippians 4:6: "Do not fret or have any anxiety about anything, but in every circumstance and in everything, by prayer and petition (definite requests), with thanksgiving, continue to make your wants known to God." Notice that it says to make "definite requests."

I have given this quite a bit of thought and realized that sometimes we are vague about what we ask God to do when we pray. We may say, "Bless me, Lord," or "Take away this problem, Father." And, of course, God knows exactly what we need before we even ask Him. But perhaps we would benefit more if we were more definite about what we need.

Let's take the example of my situation with my eyes. I could simply say, "God, please help me with my eyes," or

"Lord, heal my eyes." But when I prayed about it, I said, "Father, I need Your miracle-working power because the situation with my eyes is impossible with man, but I know all things are possible with You. As You know, Lord, my eyes are already extremely dry. I need cataract surgery and have been told that it will make them even drier. Please show me if there is anything You want me to do, and give me the miracle I need. In Jesus' name. Amen."

God has shown me two things I can do about my dry eyes, and I have done them. Now I am waiting on Him to do what only He can do. When worry, anxiety, or fear about the upcoming surgery tries to creep into my heart, I pray and say, "Father, I have turned the need concerning my eyes over to You, and I believe You will help me."[12]

I do recommend that you be definite about what you ask God to do. He is able to do exceedingly, abundantly, above and beyond anything we ask or think (Ephesians 3:20), so be bold in your prayers and don't be afraid to ask for a lot. Asking God for a lot and getting only a little of it is better than asking for a little and getting it all. He wants to do great things in our lives, but we must ask Him for them in faith.

Asking God for a lot and getting only a little is better than asking for a little and getting it all.

We often reach a place of peace concerning our need, and then Satan comes again and tries to fill our hearts with doubt and fear, wanting us to worry. When we worry long enough, we become anxious, and the devil delights in that. However, immediate prayer drives the devil away.

In addition, reminding ourselves that we have given the problem to God and that He is working on it helps to keep us calm.

I don't know exactly what God will do about the situation with my eyes, but I do totally believe that He will do something, or He will give me the grace to handle the dryness until my eyes improve. When I feel afraid, I put my trust in Him (Psalm 56:3). We should remember that when we pray, God doesn't always make our problem disappear, and when He doesn't, He will give us extra strength to handle it. We should be satisfied with the answer He gives, trusting that He knows what is best for us.

When you pray, God gives you the strength to handle your problem.

The Problem of Unforgiveness

I mentioned Mark 11:24 earlier, which tells us that whatever we ask for in prayer, if we believe we have received it, it will be ours. The following verse says, "And when you stand praying, if you hold anything against anyone, forgive them, so that your Father in heaven may forgive you your sins" (Mark 11:25).

The promise of answered prayer comes with a condition: We must forgive anyone we hold anything against. The words *anyone* and *anything* leave no room for things that we don't think are fair or things we think people don't deserve. Our part is to forgive others, just as our heavenly Father forgives us. If we refuse to do this, then our prayer won't be answered.

I never tire of teaching about unforgiveness, because I continually see how many people sacrifice answers to their prayers in order to hang on to bitterness that only poisons their life and doesn't change the one who hurt them.

God certainly doesn't ask us to forgive others more than He has been willing to forgive us. In requiring us to forgive, He is actually trying to help us, because when we harbor unforgiveness, bitterness, or resentment in our heart, it poisons our lives and we are imprisoned in our ugly thoughts. They make us angry and sad, and they do no good at all. If you have anything against anyone, I encourage you to let it go and give God an opportunity to show Himself strong in your life.

CHAPTER 5

Simple Prayer

Any concern too small to be turned into a prayer is too small to be made into a burden.

Corrie Ten Boom[13]

Prayer is such an effective weapon against anxiety, but some people fail to pray much, if at all, because they see prayer as a complicated exercise or something they don't know how to do. But I remind you: Prayer is simply talking to God about whatever is on your heart. I like to begin my prayers with praise and thanksgiving for God's goodness, and I thank Him for specific ways He has answered my previous prayers. I pray for people I know who are sick or have other problems, and then I ask God to help me with my day and anything else I need help with. However, the Bible offers no specific rules regarding prayer.

Prayer is talking to God about whatever is on your heart.

James 5:16 says, "The earnest (heartfelt, continued) prayer of a righteous man makes tremendous power available [dynamic in its working]" (AMPC).

Don't try to sound religious when you pray; just be yourself. Embrace your uniqueness, and always remember that you don't have to pray like anyone else prays. The length of your prayer is not as important as its sincerity. You can pray anytime, anywhere, about anything. A sincere, heartfelt one-minute prayer can be more powerful than thirty minutes of repetition that means very little to you.

The Model for Simple Prayer

When Jesus' disciples asked Him to teach them to pray, He gave them what we call the Lord's Prayer. It is a short and simple prayer you can use as a guideline to follow when you pray if you desire to do so.

> Our Father which art in heaven, hallowed be thy name. Thy kingdom come, Thy will be done in earth, as it is in heaven. Give us this day our daily bread. And forgive us our debts, as we forgive our debtors. And lead us not into temptation, but deliver us from evil: For thine is the kingdom, and the power, and the glory, for ever. Amen.
>
> Matthew 6:9–13 (KJV)

Let's look at each section of this prayer and learn from it.

First, the Lord's Prayer reminds us that God is our Father and that His name is holy. We should never use God's name frivolously or in a useless way. The third of the Ten Commandments states that we are not to take the Lord's name in vain (Exodus 20:7 NKJV), meaning to speak it casually or flippantly without respect for Him, or to speak it without sincerity.

The Lord's Prayer reminds us that God is our Father and His name is holy.

Next, we pray for His Kingdom to come and for His will to be done here on earth as it is in heaven. It is always good to ask God to help us do His will at all times.

"Give us this day our daily bread" is a simple statement asking God to provide for us and meet all our needs each day.

"And forgive us our debts, as we forgive our debtors" is also rendered "Forgive us our trespasses, as we forgive those who trespass against us" in some Bible translations and as "Forgive us our sins, as we have forgiven those who sin against us" in others. This is a powerful statement. We are not merely asking God to forgive our sins, but to do it *as we forgive others.* Many people ask God to forgive their sins, yet they hold unforgiveness against others. Remember, God says in His Word that if we don't forgive others, then He won't forgive us our failings and shortcomings (Mark 11:26 AMPC). We should take this very seriously. Satan gains a great deal of ground in the lives of many Christians due to their harboring unforgiveness toward another person.

Then, we ask God not to lead us into temptation. Although God never tempts us to sin, this is a way of saying, "God, keep me from temptation," or "God, help me resist temptation."

Next, the Lord's Prayer says "deliver us from evil." The world is filled with evil people who do evil deeds. Asking God to keep us safe from them is a wise thing to do.

In the King James Version of the Bible, this prayer ends with "For thine is the kingdom, and the power, and the glory, for ever. Amen." Some Bible translations don't include this sentence as part of the Lord's Prayer. However, these words powerfully

Jesus did not teach His disciples long and complicated prayers.

communicate truth to me: The kingdom is His, the power is His, and the glory is His!

If God wanted us to pray long and complicated prayers, surely Jesus would have done so when teaching His disciples to pray, but His prayer was simple and short. All prayers don't need to be short. They can be as lengthy as you want them to be, as long as they are sincere and not just repeating certain phrases for no reason. But neither do they need to be lengthy. I recall a time many years ago when God was teaching me about prayer, and He challenged me to ask Him for what I wanted in the fewest words possible. When I did, I found it to be quite powerful and liberating. Matthew 6 includes not only the Lord's Prayer, but also instructions about how we should pray. Preceding the Lord's Prayer, Jesus says we should not be "like the hypocrites, for they love to pray standing in the synagogues and on the corners of the streets," so people will see them (Matthew 6:5 AMPC). He goes on to say in this verse that people who call attention to themselves when they pray "have their reward in full already." Instead, Jesus says, "But when you pray, go into your [most] private room, and, closing the door, pray to your Father, Who is in secret; and your Father, Who sees in secret, will reward you in the open" (Matthew 6:6 AMPC).

In Matthew 6:7, Jesus continues, saying, "And when you pray, do not heap up phrases (multiply words, repeating the same ones over and over) as the Gentiles do, for they think they will be heard for their much speaking" (AMPC). There is no power in vain repetition, but God is always listening to sincere, heartfelt prayer.

Prayer and Love

Even the simplest prayer opens the door for God to work in our lives and in the lives of those we pray for. God's working in partnership with people is most

> Even the simplest prayer opens the door for God to work in your life.

amazing. He can do anything He wishes to do and certainly doesn't need our help. However, throughout the Bible, He tells us to pray. We also know that His Word says we do not have certain things because we do not ask Him for them (James 4:2). Matthew 7:7–8 teaches us that when we ask, we will receive; when we seek, we will find; when we knock, the door will be opened. So, it stands to reason that if we don't ask, seek, and knock, then we won't receive, find, or have doors opened to us.

Jesus promises that we can do the works He did and even greater works through the power of prayer (John 14:11–14). I must admit that even though I see this written plainly in God's Word, it is difficult to believe that you or I could do even greater works than Jesus did. But if Jesus said it, then it must be true. It is up to us to believe it.

When we come to God we must come in faith. Only faith pleases Him (Hebrews 11:6), and only prayers prayed in faith please Him and receive answers. Galatians 5:6 teaches us that faith works through love: "The only thing that counts is faith expressing itself through love." This shows us another secret to answered prayer—that we must be walking in love with people. We have already learned that if we harbor unforgiveness against anyone, God won't answer our prayers, and forgiveness is part of love. We pray in faith, but we need love to back up our prayers. Faith without love is like having a lamp that is not plugged in and then wondering why it won't emit light.

We need love to back up our prayers.

Here are some important truths to remember about love:

- We are to love God above everything else and then have fervent love for other people (Matthew 22:37–39).
- Faith works through love (Galatians 5:6).
- First Corinthians 13:4–8 describes exactly what love is: "Love is patient, love is kind. It does not envy, it does not boast, it is not proud. It does not dishonor others, it is not self-seeking, it is not easily angered, it keeps no record of wrongs. Love does not delight in evil but rejoices with the truth. It always protects, always trusts, always hopes, always perseveres. Love never fails."
- Love does not abuse anyone, gossip, or treat people unkindly (2 Timothy 3:1–5; Titus 3:2; Ephesians 4:29–32).
- Without the love of God flowing in our lives, our ability to help others effectively may be hindered (1 John 4:19–21).
- Love does not hoard or cling to things. One of the best ways to express love is to give to and be a blessing to others by meeting their needs (Proverbs 11:24–26; 22:9).

- Love does not play favorites or act snobbish, but values everyone (James 2:1–8).

- When we walk in love, we treat others the way we want to be treated (Luke 6:31).

- People who walk in love never quit, and they don't give up on others (Ephesians 4:2).

- Love believes the best of every person and does not judge people critically (Matthew 7:1; Romans 12:10).

Walking in love is very important to answered prayer, so please
make it a priority in your life.

> *Interpret Scripture in light of Scripture.*

Study love diligently, learn everything you can learn about it, and show it in every way you can.

While it is true that Jesus says several times that He will do whatever we ask in His name (John 14:13–14; 15:16; 16:23–24), we must interpret Scripture in light of Scripture, meaning that we must consider all of Scripture in order to gain an accurate understanding of it. Pulling one Scripture verse out of the Bible and using it without considering the others can be dangerous. A good example of this is that many people quote half of James 4:7, which in its entirety says: "Submit yourselves, then, to God. Resist the devil, and he will flee from you." But I have heard multiple people say nothing more than "Resist the devil, and he will flee." According to the whole verse, he won't flee if we are not submitted to God.

Even though Jesus says He will do whatever we ask in His name, there are other things we must consider concerning prayer. For example, we must pray according to God's will:

This is the confidence we have in approaching
God: that if we ask anything according to his will,
he hears us. And if we know that he hears us—
whatever we ask—we know that we have what we
asked of him.

1 John 5:14–15

The Bible clearly teaches that some things are God's
will and some are not. There are many things we may pray
about that may not be God's will, so it is wise to pray and
then say, "I ask this, Lord, if it is Your will."

God certainly answers prayer, and we don't need to be
perfect or to pray seemingly perfect prayers to have our
prayers answered. But there are conditions for answered
prayer, and I'd like to remind you of them:

1. We must forgive anyone that we hold anything
   against.
2. We need to pray sincerely.
3. We need to ask if we want to receive.
4. We must pray in faith.
5. We need to be living a lifestyle of loving God and
   loving people.
6. We must pray according to God's will.

CHAPTER 6

The Comfort of Prayer

Praise be to the God and Father of our Lord Jesus Christ, the Father of compassion and the God of all comfort, who comforts us in all our troubles, so that we can comfort those in any trouble with the comfort we ourselves receive from God.

2 Corinthians 1:3–4

God is the God of all comfort, and the way to receive His comfort is to ask for it. Over the years, I have learned to immediately ask God to comfort me when I get hurt in any way, and this has been very helpful to me.

When I am anxious or worried about a problem that comes up, the sooner I release the care of it to God, the sooner I receive comfort from Him. Remember, to be anxious or worried is to take on the care of a problem or a situation. We think we have to fix a problem, so we worry about what we should do. The more we worry, the more anxious we become. I tend to be a "rescuer," and if you are the same way, then you know that when you hear of a problem, even if it isn't your problem, you are tempted to go to work immediately trying to rescue whoever is hurting. Wanting to help people is noble, but we must be careful not to get in God's way. He doesn't always want to rescue people immediately. There are times when He waits in order to teach someone a deeper lesson that can only be learned by going through something unpleasant.

Be careful to not get in God's way.

In fact, a woman just told me recently that her son didn't grow up and take responsibility for his life until she stopped rescuing him from every difficulty and started allowing him to go through some difficult things.

Casting Your Care on God

First Peter 5:7 (AMP) says to cast "all your cares [all your anxieties, all your worries, and all your concerns, once and for all] on Him, for He cares about you [with deepest affection, and watches over you very carefully]." This is a tremendously powerful scripture, and it is absolutely true. God wants to take our cares, but we must be willing to give them to Him. Even after we have given our cares to Him, the enemy will certainly try to give them back to us, so we must be determined not to pick them up again. To cast your cares means to pitch or throw them away, as someone who is fishing would cast a line. God invites us to pitch our concerns to Him, to throw them on Him. He can handle them with ease, but we cannot handle them with any amount of struggle or effort.

It is God's will that you be at peace, be comfortable, and enjoy your life. This can only occur when you learn how to release your burdens to Him.

> Cast your burden on the Lord [releasing the weight of it] and He will sustain you; He will never allow the [consistently] righteous to be moved (made to slip, fall, or fail).
>
> Psalm 55:22 AMPC

Anxiety is caused by continually trying to solve problems you cannot solve. One of the most comforting

sections of Scripture to meditate on when you are tempted
to be anxious or worry is Matthew 11:28–29 (AMPC):

> Come to Me, all you who labor and are heavy-laden
> and overburdened, and I will cause you to rest. [I
> will ease and relieve and refresh your souls.] Take
> My yoke upon you and learn of Me, for I am gentle
> (meek) and humble (lowly) in heart, and you will
> find rest (relief and ease and refreshment and
> recreation and blessed quiet) for your souls.

I have turned to this Scripture passage many times
when I am having problems and have found comfort in
these verses.

Prayer and meditating on or reading specific scriptures
will definitely comfort you in times of trouble or difficulty.
When you are worried or anxious, the sooner you find
comfort, the better you will feel.

My goal in this book is to give you the answer to anxiety. I have had anxiety in my life, and I know it is certainly
not enjoyable. It is not God's will
for you. He wants you to enjoy
peace at all times, and I pray that
the lessons and insights I share
in this book are beginning to

*Anxiety is not
enjoyable, and it is not
God's will for you.*

help you. They are simple, but many of God's answers are
so simple that we miss them because we are looking for
something more complicated.

Praying for Others

Intercession, or praying for others, actually decreases anxiety and worry simply because you have your mind on someone else and their problem rather than on yourself and your problems. The less you think about your problems, the less anxious and worried you will feel. I am sure that at any given time, you know several people facing problems of some kind, and they could use your prayers. Pray specifically for God to comfort them, strengthen them, and meet whatever needs they have. Pray for them to be patient, not to give up, and to have wisdom to know what God wants them to do, if He wants them to do anything.

> *The less you think about your problems, the less anxious you will feel.*

When people are sick, ask God to heal them and remember that He often works through modern medicine and medical technology, which He has given people the knowledge and skill to create. Pray that if people you know need medical attention, they will have the wisdom to know which doctor to see, and pray that the doctor knows exactly what to do for them.

Interceding for others is very important. The Bible says that we reap what we sow (Galatians 6:7–9), and I believe that if we sow prayers for others, God will touch the hearts of many people to pray for us. Your prayers are more powerful than you may realize, and other people's prayers for you are more important than you may ever know. I appreciate tremendously the people who pray for me. I sometimes meet people who tell me they pray for me every day. This amazes me. I didn't know they had been praying, but I am sure their prayers have helped me more than I could imagine.

Hindrances to Answered Prayer

At the end of the previous chapter, I listed several conditions for answered prayer, but we also need to know what hinders answered prayer so we can make sure our prayers are answered. If I have a problem that worries me and makes me anxious, and I pray, as Paul instructs in Philippians 4:6, to get rid of anxiety, then I certainly want to make sure my prayers are not hindered. Consider how the following things can hinder the effectiveness of our prayers.

Prayerlessness

This may seem obvious, but it is worth noting that if we don't pray, our prayers cannot be answered. I remind you of James 4:2: "You do

> *If you don't pray, your prayers cannot be answered.*

not have because you do not ask God." Be sure you don't merely assume God will help you overcome anxiety, but ask Him to help you not to worry and to stay calm. God is ready to act on our behalf if we will only pray. He says in Isaiah 65:1: "I was [ready to be] inquired of by those who asked not; I was [ready to be] found by those who sought Me not. I said, Here I am, here I am [says I Am] to a nation [Israel] that has not called on My name" (AMPC).

I once had an employee who complained constantly about one thing or another, and this behavior irritated me. I fussed and fumed over the situation, and I ended up complaining about the employee who was complaining. Then I realized I had never once prayed about the situation. I simply asked God to cause the man to stop complaining about his workload and to be positive and thankful. The very next day, when I saw him, he made the first positive comment I had heard from him about his job in a long time. This is a great example of how we can fall into Satan's trap of complaining about things because we aren't praying about them.

Don't let prayerlessness hinder God from working in your life and the lives of the people you care about.

Lack of Boldness

God's Word tells us to come boldly to the throne of His grace to receive the help we need (Hebrews 4:16). Because God loves us, He doesn't want us to be afraid to approach Him in Jesus' name. We do not approach Him based on our goodness, but on the ground of what Jesus has done for us. John 14:13 teaches us that when we pray in Jesus' name, we are presenting to God all that Jesus is (AMPC). Thankfully, we do not present what we are. If we did, we would never get anything.

God wants you to ask for things that are even bigger than you can imagine. "Eye has not seen, nor ear heard...the things which God has prepared for those who

> God wants you to ask for things that are bigger than you can imagine.

love Him" (1 Corinthians 2:9 NKJV). Think about this. God has more good things stored up for us than we can even imagine.

Why does God want us to be bold? Boldness is a sign of confidence and faith, and we must approach God with both. We know that God can do great things, but we often fail to believe that He will do them *for us*. This is because we often focus on what we have done wrong, instead of seeing ourselves "in Christ" and remembering all He has done right for us. We can approach God in prayer boldly, expecting to receive answers because of what Jesus has done for us.

Hidden Sin

We all have sin in our lives, but if we repent of our sins, God forgives them and removes them as far as the east is from the west (Psalm 103:12). Psalm 66:18 says,

> If you refuse to deal with your sins, God will not answer your prayers.

"If I regard iniquity in my heart, the Lord will not hear me" (AMPC). In other words, if we refuse to deal with our sins, God will not answer our prayers. If we harbor hidden sin in our hearts, we cannot pray with boldness.

Praying outside of God's Will

We have already established that God won't hear prayers that are not in accordance with His will, but it is good to go over this fact again. Sometimes when I pray and I am not sure that what I'm asking for is God's will, I add, "and Lord, please don't give it to me unless it is Your will." Having or doing things that are not God's will is a heavy burden. He will help us do anything that is His will, but if we try to do things that are not His will, then we will struggle and experience a great deal of anxiety.

Praying with Wrong Motives

We know that James 4:2 says we don't have because we don't ask God, but James 4:3 goes on to say that if we ask with "wrong motives," we won't receive. In other words, we will not receive what we ask for if we intend to use it in the wrong manner.

Many people never think about their motives, but motives are very important to God. A motive is what I call "the why behind the what." God is more concerned with why we do something than with what we are doing. Our motives should be pure. Selfishness is a wrong motive. I must admit that there were years when I prayed for my ministry to grow because I thought the bigger it was, the more important I would be. And guess what?

Motives are very important to God.

God didn't answer my prayers until I saw the truth and repented for my wrong motive. My ministry didn't grow until my true desire was to help hurting people and fulfill God's call on my life. I encourage you today to take some time and really examine the motives behind what you do, and you may find some things that will help you.

Doubt and Unbelief

We know that faith in God is foundational to answered prayer, so it stands to reason that doubt and unbelief—the opposites of faith—would hinder answered prayer. I am always impressed with the man who told Jesus, "I believe; help my unbelief!" (Mark 9:24 NKJV). He was honest with Jesus and still received his miracle. Keep your eyes off everything that will steal your faith and do as Hebrews 12:2 says, "[looking away from all that will distract us and] focusing our eyes on Jesus, who is the Author and Perfecter of faith" (AMP).

Avoid listening to people who have no faith and try to steal your faith through being negative or telling you the natural reasons that what you are believing for cannot happen. When Jesus went to raise Jairus's daughter from the dead, He didn't take all twelve disciples into the room with Him; He took only Peter, James, and John (Mark 5:21–24, 35–43). We don't know for sure why He only took those three, but perhaps it was because He wanted to be surrounded by the ones who had the most faith.

Worry

Pray your worries instead of worrying your prayers. In other words, pray about the things that worry you and cause you anxiety, but after you have prayed, don't keep worrying. Praying but continuing to worry does not demonstrate faith in God. Take your hands and your mind off your troublesome situations and give them completely to Him. Every time you feel yourself being drawn back into a problem, resist the temptation to revisit it and remember that you have given the problem to God.

Unforgiveness

Although I wrote in chapter 4 about the importance of forgiving anyone you have anything against, I want to remind you here of how important it is. Paul writes in Ephesians 4:26–27 that we should not let the sun go down on our anger or we will give the devil a foothold in our lives. Be sure you never forget how important it is to forgive quickly and completely.

Never forget how important it is to forgive quickly and completely.

Pride

Pride makes us think we can solve our own problems. God helps the humble, but He sets Himself against the proud, or He "resists" the proud, according to 1 Peter 5:5–7 (AMPC):

For God sets Himself against the proud (the insolent, the overbearing, the disdainful, the presumptuous, the boastful)—[and He opposes, frustrates, and defeats them], but gives grace (favor, blessing) to the humble. Therefore, humble yourselves [demote, lower yourselves in your own estimation] under the mighty hand of God, that in due time He may exalt you, casting the whole of your care [all your anxieties, all your worries, all your concerns, once and for all] on Him, for He cares for you affectionately and cares about you watchfully.

This Scripture passage was extremely helpful to me as I was learning to cast my care on God. It is only pride that causes us to think we can solve our problems without God's help. Before I learned to cast my care on Him, I felt frustrated because nothing I did seemed to work, and these verses taught me that it was actually God resisting me because of my pride and that He would not help me until I humbled myself and admitted that I could not help myself. I had to learn to cast my cares on Him and let Him take care of me.

I know that letting go of what concerns us may be scary because of bad experiences that caused us to think we cannot trust people, but God is not like people at all. He always does what He says He will do. If we cast our care on Him, He will take care of us.

Pray, cast your care on God, and let the Scripture and the Holy Spirit, who is the Comforter, comfort you in whatever painful and troublesome situation you are facing.

CHAPTER 7

With Thanksgiving

Appreciation can make a day, even change a life. Your willingness to put it into words is all that is necessary.

Margaret Cousins[14]

Living with a thankful heart, no matter what is taking place in our lives at the moment, like prayer, is vitally important to overcoming worry and anxiety. Remember that Philippians 4:6 tells us to pray *with thanksgiving* in order to obtain the peace that passes understanding. Let's explore the power and discipline of thanksgiving in this chapter and the next one.

Psalm 100:4 says, "Be thankful and say so" (AMPC). This scripture contains a powerful message. We may think we are thankful, but the real power is in saying so. William Arthur Ward said, "Feeling gratitude and not expressing it is like wrapping a present and not giving it."[15] He also said: "God gave you a gift of 86,400 seconds today. Have you used one to say thank you?"[16] This is a good question for all of us to consider.

People cannot read our minds, so they need to hear our words, especially words of gratitude. Being thankful releases power in

> People cannot read your mind, so they need to hear your words.

our life, and saying we are thankful to God is extremely important. Telling people we are thankful encourages them and even strengthens them. We cannot say thank you too often. Expressing gratitude keeps us from developing an attitude of entitlement. We don't ever want to take what God does for us or what people do for us for granted and let these kindnesses become expectations instead of blessings we appreciate.

People frequently ask, "What is God's will for my life?" There are other aspects to finding God's total and specific will for each of us, but 1 Thessalonians 5:18 teaches us that God's will to give thanks is for everyone: "Give thanks in all circumstances; for this is God's will for you in Christ Jesus." If you are searching for God's will for your life, giving thanks in all circumstances is a good place to begin. As you continue in thanksgiving, more of His specific desires for your life will be revealed to you.

Giving thanks has a powerful effect in the spiritual realm. Satan doesn't want us to be thankful. He wants us to murmur, complain, and be discontent, because these attitudes and behaviors open a door for him to work in our lives. In the same way, I believe gratitude opens a door for God to work in our lives.

The Israelites were instructed to give "thank offerings," at certain times (2 Chronicles 29:31, 33:16; Psalm 107:22), and I think this is a great idea. In addition to your regular giving, why not consider giving something special just because you want to say "Thank You, God, for Your goodness in my life."

When you notice what you have to be thankful for, you stop noticing what you lack.

When we notice what we have to be thankful for, we stop noticing what we lack. I believe an attitude of gratitude shows that we are developing godly character.

Are You Focused on Your Blessings or Your Problems?

Whatever we focus on becomes the biggest thing in our life. If we focus on it long enough, it may even become the only situation we see. We are all blessed, and people who think they aren't blessed are not seeing clearly. They may have focused for so long on what is wrong in their life, that they have lost their capacity to see the blessings they do have. Hannah Whitall Smith wrote, "The soul that gives thanks can find comfort in everything; the soul that complains can find comfort in nothing."[17]

I recall a time when I was unhappy with Dave. I thought over and over about the things he did that aggravated me, and God challenged me to make a list of what bothered me about Dave and a list of what I liked about him. To my surprise, when I finished both lists, the one about things I liked about Dave was much longer than the one about what I didn't like. If you are having problems with someone in your life, consider making these lists, and you just may find that the benefits of this person far outweigh the problems.

Most of us have heard that we should count our blessings, and it might be a very good idea to do just that. Try counting yours, and you will probably grow weary of counting before you run out of blessings. Remember, Philippians 4:6 tells us to pray about our needs and to be thankful instead of being anxious. Being thankful will distract us from our anxieties.

Being thankful will distract you from your anxieties.

I realize that writing about being thankful when you have problems is much easier than doing it. As a matter of fact, I had an unexpected situation come up last evening that really upset me, so I had to apply this message to myself. It was difficult because my emotions were involved, but when I am writing or teaching, they are not involved. As I write, it has been about eighteen hours since the situation came up. I am about 80 percent of the way to victory and will need to keep pressing on until I get complete victory over this circumstance. Even after that, I am sure thoughts about what happened will revisit me, and I will have to renew my commitment to pray and be thankful instead of being anxious and worried.

If you have a big problem in your life right now, pray about the situation and then spend a few moments thinking about the many things God provides to us each day, such as peace, answered prayer, grace, forgiveness of sin, new beginnings, mercy, hope, and right relationship with Him through Christ. He helps us, He is with us all the time, and He gives us strength and wisdom, to name just a few of our blessings. Jesus says that we will experience tribulation (difficulties) in the world (John 16:33), but we have God's Word to help us. Just imagine how awful it is for people who have problems and don't have God's help.

The apostle Paul included many prayers in his letters, but I can't find anywhere where he prayed for anyone's problems to go away. He did pray, however, that they would bear whatever came with a good attitude. Having a good attitude and gratitude during difficulty is a sign of spiritual maturity, and God calls us to mature into the likeness of Jesus. Paul writes in Ephesians 5:1, "Therefore be imitators of God, as beloved children" (ESV). In Romans 8:29, he writes, "For those whom he foreknew he also predestined to be conformed to the image of his Son, in order that he might be the firstborn among many brothers" (ESV).

We are to follow in the footsteps of Jesus. He regularly gave thanks to God and never complained, not even when He went to the cross and suffered for our sins.

Do You Give Thanks More Than You Complain, or Complain More Than You Give Thanks?

In Paul's short letter to the Colossians, I found four times when he instructs the people to give thanks (2:6–7; 3:15, 17; 4:2). No one has to tell us to complain. It is a natural tendency of human nature, but we frequently need to be reminded to give thanks.

I heard a story about a homeless man who was often hungry, cold, and tired. He was in poor health and had no family to love him. Although this man often had to find scraps for himself to eat, he always fed the birds some of what he had. When asked how he felt about being homeless, he replied, "I have air in my lungs and I'm grateful for everything I have been blessed with. I am especially grateful for three things: I'm alive, I have the ability to love, and I have my beloved birds."

This is a pretty amazing story. This homeless man was more thankful for the very little he had than most of us are for the abundance we enjoy. We should let his example challenge us to grow in this area.

Dietrich Bonhoeffer wrote in his book *Life Together*:

> In the Christian community thankfulness is just what it is anywhere else in the Christian life. Only he who gives thanks for little things receives the big things. We prevent God from giving us the great spiritual gifts He has in store for us, because we do not give thanks for daily gifts. We think we dare not be satisfied with the small measure of spiritual knowledge, experience, and love that has been given to us, and that we must constantly be looking forward eagerly for the highest good. Then we deplore the fact that we lack the deep certainty, the strong faith, and the rich experience that God has given to others, and we consider this lament to be pious. We pray for the big things and forget to give thanks for the ordinary, small (and yet really not small) gifts. How can God entrust great things to one who will not thankfully receive from Him the little things? If we do not give thanks daily for the Christian fellowship in which we have been placed, even where there is no great experience, no discoverable riches, but much weakness, small

faith, and difficulty; if on the contrary, we only keep complaining to God that everything is so paltry and petty, so far from what we expected, then we hinder God from letting our fellowship grow according to the measure and riches which are there for us all in Jesus Christ.[18]

God answers prayers, but He doesn't answer complaints. This is why Philippians 4:6 teaches

> God answers prayers, not complaints.

us to pray with thanksgiving. Complaining is the voice of a lack of appreciation for what we do have. In 1 Thessalonians 5, immediately after we read in verse 18 that we are to "give thanks in all circumstances; for this is God's will for you in Christ Jesus," we read in verse 19, "Do not quench the Spirit." *To quench* means to stop or put out, and I believe complaining does quench the Spirit.

We are to do everything "without grumbling or arguing," according to Philippians 2:14. The next verse, Philippians 2:15, states that if we will eliminate these habits from our lives, we will be seen like stars shining brightly in a "warped and crooked generation." Everywhere I go I hear people complaining, but when I meet someone who is thankful, I always think, *I'll bet that person is a Christian.* Why? Because they are behaving as the Bible teaches Christians to behave.

Can you be inconvenienced without complaining? If any of us could get through one entire day without complaining about anything at all, it might fall into the category

> *Life is filled with annoyances, so you must be willing to adapt.*

of a miracle. Complaining seems to be our default button for anything that is even mildly inconvenient. Life is filled with little annoyances, and I doubt this will change, so we must be willing to adapt.

In Numbers 21:4–8, as the Israelites made their way through the wilderness, they grumbled about the manna (heavenly bread) that God gave them each day, and they complained about a lack of water, although God had previously performed the miracle of giving them water from a rock (Numbers 20:8–11). They blamed everything uncomfortable on Moses and even on God (Numbers 21:5). Their complaining opened the door for venomous snakes to get into their camp and many people fell dead in a single day. Finally, they said to Moses, "We sinned when we spoke against the Lord and against you. Pray that the Lord will take the snakes away from us" (v. 7). So Moses prayed, and God answered his prayer. It is a shame that so many people had to die before they realized and admitted they had sinned and asked Moses to pray for them. Yes, complaining is sin. Perhaps you have never seen it this way, but it is. Romans 14:23 teaches us that whatever is not of faith is sin, and I doubt that any of us complain by faith. Billy Graham said, "Grumbling and gratitude are, for the child of God, in conflict. Be grateful and you won't grumble. Grumble and you won't be grateful."[19]

Complaining was one reason it took the Israelites forty years to make what was actually an eleven-day journey through the wilderness. Their immaturity was a sign they were not ready for the Promised Land, because in order to possess the land, they had to first dispossess those who currently occupied it (Deuteronomy 9:1, 11:23). In other words, they had to fight for what God had given them.

We also must be ready to fight for what God has given us. Everything that Jesus died for us to have, Satan will try to prevent us from taking. We can defeat Satan if we are thankful to God and say so, but we cannot defeat him with complaining and grumbling. We can certainly talk openly to God about how we feel in the midst of our difficulties, but we should also voice our thankfulness and trust in Him.

Are You Willing to Do Something about It?

Don't complain about something you are not willing to do something about. For example, do you complain about your schedule and how busy you are? I did until

> Don't complain about something you're not willing to do something about.

God told me that I made my schedule and could change it if I wanted to. I said yes to too many things in an effort to please people, and I needed to learn to say no when I knew saying yes would put too much stress on me. If we wear ourselves out, don't get adequate sleep, and live under continual stress, then we cannot complain when we get sick.

Do you complain about your bills and debt? If so, remember that you are the one who spent the money, and if you don't respect money, then don't expect money. Don't buy things you can't pay for and then complain because you have the pressure of debt. God's Word tells us to "owe nothing to anyone except to love one another" (Romans 13:8 NASB).

Nehemiah was grieved about the broken-down walls in Jerusalem, but he also had a vision to rebuild them and worked hard to do so (Nehemiah 1–6). Habakkuk had a complaint, and God told him to get a vision and write it down so plainly that everyone who passed by could see it (Habakkuk 2:1–2).

If you have a complaint or grievance, get a vision to fix the problem instead of complaining and blaming others. We cannot complain our way into a better life. Complaining is a total waste of time and does no good at all.

> You cannot complain your way into a better life.

The Sacrifice of Praise

We may not always feel thankful, but we can still offer a sacrifice of praise to God (Hebrews 13:15). Under the Old Covenant, the Israelites had to offer the dead bodies of animals as their sacrifices, but under the New Covenant we get to offer thanksgiving and praise. As hard as being thankful and praising God may be sometimes, it is still easier than what the Israelites had to do. No matter

> No matter how many problems you have, you are still blessed beyond understanding.

how many annoying problems we have, God is still good and we are blessed beyond understanding.

Jesus Notices

In Luke 17:11–13, Jesus is on His way to Jerusalem. As He passes between Samaria and Galilee, He comes across ten lepers, who stand at a distance and cry, "Jesus, Master, have mercy on us" (v. 13 ESV). Let's look at what happens next:

> When he saw them he said to them, "Go and show yourselves to the priests." And as they went they were cleansed. Then one of them, when he saw that he was healed, turned back, praising God with a loud voice; and he fell on his face at Jesus' feet, giving him thanks. Now he was a Samaritan. Then Jesus answered, "Were not ten cleansed? Where are the nine? Was no one found to return and give praise to God except this foreigner?" And he said to him, "Rise and go your way; your faith has made you well."
>
> Luke 17:14–19 ESV

Jesus noticed that nine of the ten former lepers didn't bother to come back and give thanks for their healing. This means that 90 percent of those He healed did not express their gratitude for what He had done. I can't help but wonder what happened to those nine. I do pray that this is not an accurate statistic for how many people don't bother to thank God for His goodness in their life. We may need to think about the fact that God sees everything we do. He is everywhere all the time, and He knows all things. When we don't give thanks, Jesus notices.

All Things Work Together for Good

One big reason we can give thanks in all things is that God's promise in Romans 8:28 is true: "And we know that in all things God works for the good of those who love him, who have been called according to his purpose." If we believe God's Word and trust Him, we can give thanks in all things with ease because we believe that even though the things we are currently experiencing may not be good, God can work them together with other things and make them good.

In the Old Testament, even though Joseph's brothers had treated him horribly, he told them that what they had intended for harm, God intended for good (Genesis 50:20). Even the sexual abuse I endured throughout my childhood has worked for the good of many people, because as God healed and delivered me from the effects of the abuse, I have been able to share with others who have been abused, and they have been encouraged that God will heal and deliver them too. Trust God and let Him use your pain for someone else's gain. This is the way to defeat the devil. We overcome evil with good (Romans 12:21).

No matter what kind of problem you experience in life,

if you will trust God to work it
out for good, you will be amazed
what He will do. Believing this

> *Trust God to work out your problems.*

will help you give thanks in the midst of difficulty. You
know that it won't last forever and that it will end well.

Find the Good in Everything

Are you an optimist or a pessimist? Our lives are made miserable or enjoyable not based on
what is happening around us, but
based on our attitude toward it.

> *Your life is made miserable not by what is happening around you, but by your attitude.*

People who only see problems are
miserable, but those who find the good in situations are
happy, regardless of their circumstances.

James 1:2–4 says: "My brethren, count it all joy when you
fall into various trials, knowing that the testing of your faith
produces patience. But let patience have its perfect work, that
you may be perfect and complete, lacking nothing" (NKJV).

This is an amazing scripture because it tells us that,
even in the midst of trials, if we will consider (think of)
them as pure joy, they will produce patience in us. Amazingly, patience causes us to be people who lack nothing.

People who are truly patient can be happy no matter
what is happening in or around them. Paul writes that
he had "learned the secret of being content in any and
every situation," whether he lived "in plenty or in want"
(Philippians 4:12). I am encouraged by the fact that he

learned to be content. It did not come naturally to him, but he had to choose how to look at life. I too am learning to be content. I have not arrived, but I am pressing on.

Trials, by nature, are difficult, but they are good for us because they bring out what is in us, good or bad. We learn to truly know ourselves during hard times. I often say that trials brought a lot out of me before they brought patience. As a young, immature Christian, my difficulties brought out anger, impatience, confusion, self-pity, and many other ungodly responses. But as God continued to work in my life, I did finally get to patience. I thank God for all the experiences I have had, both good and challenging, because they do all work together for good.

Kahlil Gibran said, "The optimist sees the rose and not its thorns; the pessimist stares at the thorns, oblivious to the rose."[20] Some people see their life this way. They are so focused on the thorns (difficulties) that they never see the roses (blessings).

> *We can have no appreciation for life's good times if we've never experienced difficulty.*

I have come to believe that we would have no appreciation of or gratitude for life's good times if we never experienced difficulty. Dave and I often talk about the very difficult years when we started Joyce Meyer Ministries, and we thank God for how blessed we are now.

Author and coach Marc Chernoff had a conversation with his seventy-one-year-old father about life and growing through adversity, and said this about it:

One of the last things he said before we got off the phone resonated so much with me that I wrote it down. He said, "It's been my experience that most people aren't truly happy until they've had many reasons to be sad. I believe this is because it takes all of those bad days and hardships to teach us how to truly appreciate what we have. It builds our resilience."[21]

I wholeheartedly agree. We grow spiritually during hard times, and this ultimately enables us to enjoy life all the time, regardless of our circumstances.

Be thankful for everything that comes into your life, because it all works together to make you the person God wants you to be. Regard your difficulties as joy, because you know they are working something good in you (James 1:2).

Romans 8:37 teaches us that we are more than conquerors through Christ, who loves us. I think this means that we know we have victory before our trials even begin. We live with a winner's attitude because God has already told us that we win in the end.

As I close this chapter, let me ask you to consider the Old Testament man Job, who endured terrible difficulties. His troubles were probably worse than any we have ever experienced, yet he could still say, "I know that my redeemer lives, and that in the end he will stand on the earth. And after my skin has been destroyed, yet in my flesh I will see God; I myself will see him with my own eyes—I, and not another. How my heart yearns within me!" (Job 19:25–27).

CHAPTER 8

The Discipline of Gratitude

Discipline is the bridge between goals and accomplishment.

Jim Rohn[22]

All of us would probably say that we want to be grateful, but as Jim Rohn states, discipline is the bridge between what we want to do and accomplishing it. God's Word teaches us that we should be disciplined. Even though discipline does not seem joyous when it is being applied, it will produce a "harvest of righteousness and peace" later on (Hebrews 12:11). Discipline is a habit that can be developed. It is not a quality that is inborn in us; we must train ourselves in it on purpose. When we discipline ourselves, we do what we know we should do, even though we don't feel like doing it. We can be thankful when we feel like being thankful and when we don't.

Henri Nouwen said:

> Gratitude...goes beyond the "mine" and "thine" and claims the truth that all of life is a pure gift. In the past I always thought of gratitude as a spontaneous response to the awareness of gifts received, but now I realize that gratitude can also be lived as a discipline. The discipline of gratitude is the explicit effort to acknowledge that all I am and have is given to me as a gift of love, a gift to be celebrated with joy.[23]

People who are thankful have trained and disciplined themselves to look at what they have and be amazed by the fact that God has been so generous to them. They know they don't deserve it, but they are thankful for it. They practice being thankful daily. Any misery can be made better if we maintain an attitude of gratitude. When I have a huge, unexpected, unwanted problem, my first temptation is to complain, feel sorry for myself, and worry. But through discipline, I am learning how to look away from anything that distracts me from God and His goodness and instead discipline myself to look for the blessings in my life. We can find something good in every discomfort if we will only look for it.

Any misery can be made better through gratitude.

We can discipline ourselves to look for the good in all things. A friend of mine shared this list with me:

- I am thankful to be able to get out of bed every morning, even if I am a little stiff or still sleepy, because it reminds me that I am alive and I have things to do each day.
- I am thankful when I have to cook a meal, because it reminds me that I have food to eat.
- I am thankful when I get sore from exercising, because it reminds me that I am blessed with health and strength.
- I am thankful when the oil in my car needs changing, because it reminds me that I have a car to take me where I need to go.
- I am thankful when I have to juggle invitations or opportunities to be with friends or family, because it

reminds me that I am blessed with people to love and people who love me.

- I am thankful if my clothes feel a bit tight, because that reminds me that I have plenty of food.
- I am thankful when I have to walk to another part of the house to turn off a light or to adjust the thermostat, because it reminds me that I have electricity and a comfortable home.
- I am thankful when my elderly father moves slowly and takes so long to do things that my patience wears thin, because I am reminded that he is a wonderful blessing to me.
- I am thankful when I pay bills, because it reminds me that I am able to buy what I need.
- I am thankful when I fight traffic, because it reminds me that I have somewhere to go.
- I am thankful when I have to repeat myself to people who are hard of hearing, because it reminds me that I have people in my life who are interested in what I have to say.

My friend's list includes things most of us can relate to, so next time you find yourself in one of these situations, I hope you will remember to be thankful because of what it reminds you of.

I am practicing disciplining myself to be thankful from the moment I wake up each morning. I am thankful that I can easily step out of bed and go to the bathroom without needing a wheelchair or someone to help me get there. I am thankful for warm water to wash my face. I'm thankful for my morning coffee, because I *really* like it. Recently I spilled my coffee twice in one week and made a huge mess, but I disciplined myself to be thankful that I had enough coffee to make another cup.

Look for something to be thankful for in every situation.

Once you begin looking for something to be thankful for in every situation, it becomes an enjoyable practice that tops any game a child likes to play. I look at it this way: The enemy is doing his best to get me upset and angry, but I defeat him each time I find something I can be thankful for in the midst of a problem instead of complaining about it.

I think the devil sets us up to get us upset. He uses things like spilled coffee, annoying interruptions, people who are difficult to deal with, and hundreds of other circumstances to try to upset us, but through discipline we can find a way to be thankful for something in each situation.

Pollyanna, a 1960 movie starring Hayley Mills, is the story of a cheerful orphan girl who changed a whole town through playing what she called "the glad game." She found a way to be cheerful no matter what happened, especially when something could have made her sad.

When you are thankful, it changes not only you but also the people around you.

When we discipline ourselves to be thankful and glad no matter what happens, it changes not only us, but also the people around us. If enough of us played the glad game, we might just change the world. Imagine how different the world would be if all negativity were replaced with gratitude for some blessing, whether the blessings were small or large.

If you really think about it, there are thousands of things to be thankful for, and all you have to do is discipline yourself to look for them daily. Gratitude is empowering and energizing.

What Is Self-Discipline?

Self-discipline is the ability to control yourself and to make yourself work hard or behave in a particular way without needing someone to tell you what to do.

We often hear people say, "I'm just not disciplined," but this is not a true statement, because God has given us a spirit of discipline and self-control. These scriptures tell us so:

> For the Spirit God gave us does not make us timid,
> but gives us power, love and self-discipline.
> 2 Timothy 1:7

> But the fruit of the Spirit is love, joy, peace, forbearance, kindness, goodness, faithfulness, gentleness and self-control. Against such things there is no law.
> Galatians 5:22–23

> Better a patient person than a warrior, one with
> self-control than one who takes a city.
>
> Proverbs 16:32

God's Word tells us to be like the ant, which gathers food in harvest without anyone making it do the right thing (Proverbs 6:6–8). There are at least sixteen verses in the New International Version of the Bible about self-control or self-discipline. God never tells us to do something that we cannot do; therefore, to say that we simply cannot control ourselves is not true.

To develop any habit, you have to practice it over and over.

When we are developing any habit, we have to practice it over and over. This is as true for discipline and self-control as for anything else. We can develop discipline and self-control in specific areas if we are willing to put in the effort.

As of the writing of this book, my husband has worked out with weights for sixty-three years, and I never hear him complain about doing it. Only rarely have I heard him say, "Working out today was challenging. I just didn't want to do it." This is because he has his mind set and keeps it set (Colossians 3:2 AMPC) on doing what he knows will help to keep him strong and healthy. This is an example of self-discipline. Many people have commented on how good Dave looks and said they "wish" they could look as good as he does. But he didn't get that way by wishing. It took, and continues to take, discipline and effort, both of which God gives us grace to develop if we are willing to do our part.

Self-discipline requires maturity and character. Those who are self-disciplined will realize its

> *Self-discipline requires maturity and character.*

benefits. They will end up succeeding at what they do. We might even say that discipline leads us to success.

As an employer, I enjoy employees who are self-disciplined. I don't have to follow up with anyone to make sure they do what was asked of them. Actually, there are times when they do what needs to be done before I even ask, because they look ahead and perceive what the need will be before anyone mentions it to them.

If people like this want to form a habit such as being more thankful, they will. It will take time, as it does with all new habits, but they won't give up until they develop it.

Look Around You

If you want to have more gratitude, all you need to do is look at some of the challenges other people face. Think about the peo-

> *To have more gratitude, look at the challenges other people face.*

ple who don't have jobs before you complain about yours. Or, when you are tempted to complain about a headache, think of the people who have just received a report that they have cancer and only three months to live.

When we are hurting, our first impulse isn't to look for someone who is hurting worse than we are, nor is it to look for a reason to be thankful. But this is the best thing to do, and it does please God. If we discipline ourselves to do it long enough, it will become a habit and will no longer be something we must "try" to do because it will be our normal way of responding to trials of any kind.

Writing this book is helping me because, perhaps like you, I have a few problematic situations taking place in my life right now. However, I don't have to let them discourage me, because I can be thankful on purpose. I don't have to follow my feelings or be filled with self-pity, because I have much more to be thankful for than I have to complain about. What about you? Don't you have more to be thankful for than you do to complain about? I'm sure you do, and you will find those things if you will simply look for them.

> Before you complain, look for something to be glad about.

Before you complain about anything, look around you and take time to see if you can find something to be glad about. Now, verbalize it. Verbalizing your gratitude is important for many reasons. It blesses God when we are thankful and say so, and hearing ourselves say we are thankful is helpful to us, because according to God's Word, we feed on our own words. They have consequences that affect us. Proverbs 18:20 says, "A man's [moral] self shall be filled with the fruit of his mouth; and with the consequence of his words he must be satisfied [whether good or evil]" (AMPC).

Last but not least, our words have an effect in the

spiritual realm. They minister life or death, according to Proverbs 18:21: "Death and life are in the power of the tongue, and they who indulge in it shall eat the fruit of it [for death or life]" (AMPC). They give the devil an opportunity to bring trouble through angry words we speak (Ephesians 4:26–27) or they release angels to work on our behalf because angels hearken "unto the voice of his word" (Psalm 103:20–21 KJV).

Be Committed

I want to strongly encourage you to be committed—wholeheartedly dedicated—to forming the habit of being thankful in and for all things, knowing that God is good and will work something good out of even your most anxious situation if you follow His directions.

I strongly believe that gratitude is a form of spiritual warfare. We have an enemy, Satan, often referred to as the devil. He is committed to our destruction and works hard to accomplish it, desiring to make us miserable and ungrateful. He hates it when we trust God, believe He is good, or give Him thanks for anything. But the weapons of our warfare are not carnal or fleshly; they are spiritual (2 Corinthians 10:4). Gratitude and a thankful heart are weapons that help to defeat the devil's evil plans against us.

In 2 Chronicles 20, we see that Jehoshaphat appointed singers to sing and others to praise God during a time of battle, and their praise confused and defeated the enemy. They sang, "Give thanks to the Lord, for his love endures forever" (2 Chronicles 20:21). You too can confuse the enemy by being thankful when, according to your circumstance, you should be complaining.

When anxiety and worry fill your mind and heart, you have learned the keys to having peace no matter what your circumstances are. Let me remind you of them:

1. Remember past victories.
2. Fight the good fight of faith.
3. Believe that God is in control.
4. Trust God.
5. Choose to believe how much God loves you.

CHAPTER 9

The Peace That Passes Understanding

All men desire peace, but very few desire those things that make for peace.

Thomas a Kempis[24]

Philippians 4:6–7, the Scripture passage on which this book is based, teaches us that if we will pray with thanksgiving instead of being anxious and worried, God's peace, which passes understanding, will be ours. Peace that passes understanding is peace that God gives us in the midst of life's storms. When we have it, then even when our circumstances say we should be frantic, anxious, and worried, we are at peace because we know God loves us and will care for us.

> God gives us peace that passes understanding in the midst of life's storms.

I love peace. I lived the first forty years of my life without it, and now I don't think life is worth living if we don't have it. I will do almost anything to have peace. I confront things when I need to, but I value peace so much that I am willing to give up being anxious, worried, angry, unforgiving, offended, or upset in order to have it.

I'm even willing to give up being right unless I truly need to take a stand on something important. It is amazing how many arguments we have with others in an effort to prove we are right. Being right is highly overrated, and it costs us much more than it is worth. According to Proverbs 13:10, pride causes contention and strife. If we truly desire peace, we often need to humble ourselves not only before God, but also before other people.

To be clear, I believe we should stand firm for truth, but

people tend to argue about many matters that are petty and what the Amplified Bible, Classic Edition calls "(stupid) controversies over ignorant questionings" (2 Timothy 2:23). We are to avoid these issues and humble ourselves if necessary to keep from forfeiting peace in an effort to win an argument that is not worth having.

Like most people, there was a season in my life that I prayed for peace, but it seemed to evade me most of the time. I occasionally enjoyed peace when my circumstances were calm and suitable, but that was not often. I always prayed for my circumstances to change, but I needed to pray that I would change. I needed to be stronger and more stable instead of so easily affected by circumstances.

> I prayed for my circumstances to change, but I needed to pray that I myself would change.

Peace Is Our Inheritance

Nineteenth-century evangelist Dwight L. Moody said: "A great many people are trying to make peace, but that has already been done. God has not left it for us to do; all we have to do is to enter into it."[25]

Often, we hear people say, "I've lost my peace," and this is a true statement. They have peace because Jesus has given it to us. But people lose their peace because of their circumstances, and then they need to find it again. I can remember feeling this way. I finally learned that, according to Scripture, I had peace, but I wasn't entering into it. When I prayed, it's no wonder my prayers were not answered; I was praying for something I already had. Jesus says in John 14:27 (AMPC):

> Peace I leave with you; My [own] peace I now give and bequeath to you. Not as the world gives do I give to you. Do not let your hearts be troubled, neither let them be afraid. [Stop allowing yourselves to be agitated and disturbed; and do not permit yourselves to be fearful and intimidated and cowardly and unsettled.]

Studying this scripture was a turning point for me in terms of enjoying a life of peace. I understood from it that Jesus has given me His peace. Peace was mine! I had a quality of peace unlike the peace the world offers. The world offers peace when our circumstances are pleasant, but God gives us a peace that passes understanding— peace when our circumstances are upsetting. When we have Jesus' peace, we can face troubling circumstances and still be at peace.

In order to enter into the peace Jesus gave to me, I had to stop allowing myself to be agitated and disturbed or anxious and worried. God had done His part by giving me peace, but I saw that I wasn't doing my part. I was anxious and I worried a lot. I prayed only as a last resort, after I had done everything else I knew to do, and I complained instead of being thankful. When I did pray, I prayed for my troublesome circumstance to go away instead of praying for the Holy Spirit to strengthen me on the inside so I could endure with good temper whatever came my way.

Peace—not eliminating circumstances we don't like—should be our goal, because if we have peace, it doesn't matter whether our circumstances are pleasant or unpleasant. We remain the same. Peace is not the absence of problems; it is trusting God in the midst of life's storms. Here is a story that illustrates this point:

Peace is trusting God in the midst of life's storms.

The Real Meaning of Peace

There once lived a king who announced [a] prize [for] the artist who would paint the best painting depicting peace. Many great painters sent the king several of their best art pieces. One of the pictures among the various master pieces was of a calm lake perfectly mirroring peacefully towering snow-capped mountains. [Overhead] was a blue clear sky with fluffy clouds. The picture was perfect. Most of the people who viewed the pictures of peace from various artist[s] thought that it was the best among all.

But when the king announced the winner, everyone was shocked. The picture which won the prize had mountains too[,] but it was rugged and bare. The sky looked very angry; there [was] lightning. This did not look peaceful at all. It looked like the artist had mistakenly submitted his painting depicting a storm rather than peace. But if anyone looked closely at the painting, he could see a tiny bush growing in the cracks in the rock. In the bush a mother bird had built her nest. In the midst of the rush of angry weather, the bird sat on her nest with peace.

[P]eace does not mean to be in a place where there is no noise or trouble. Peace means to be in the midst of all the chaos and still be calm in the heart. [R]eal peace is the state of mind, not the state of the surroundings. The mother bird [at peace and] calm, despite her chaotic surrounding[s,] indeed was the best representation for peace.[26]

Satan can arrange for an unpleasant circumstance, and as long as it upsets us, he wins. But when he brings upsetting things and we don't let them upset us, then he loses and we win.

St. Francis de Sales wrote, "The same everlasting Father who cares for you today will care for you tomorrow and every day. Either he will shield you from suffering or give you unfailing strength to bear it. Be at peace then and put aside all anxious thoughts and imaginations."[27]

Peace Stealers

Once I reached the point of wanting peace badly enough to let God change me instead of always asking Him to change my circumstances, I finally began to enjoy peace. I had to learn what my peace stealers were. In other words, I had to figure out what the enemy used to steal my peace. They included household items that needed repairs, which cost money, and we did not have much money. They also included unexpected doctor visits for one of the children and prescriptions that needed to be filled. In those days, we did not have the type of health insurance people have today, and what we had did not cover doctor visits and prescriptions. We had what was called hospitalization, which paid 80 percent of the hospital bills if one of us had to be hospitalized, but nothing else.

At that time, I was still an immature Christian, so it didn't take very much to upset me. I got upset if I didn't get my way or if someone didn't agree with me, if Dave wanted to play golf and I wanted him to stay home, and for other reasons. Pretty much anything that required even a little bit of patience, self-sacrifice, or inconvenience would upset me, make me anxious, and cause me to worry. Financial setbacks especially caused me to worry because I did not know how to trust God to meet our needs. One of my big peace stealers was rude, angry, and obnoxious people who were mean and unkind to me for no reason or who blamed me for their problems instead of taking personal responsibility for them. Once I began to identify my peace stealers, I worked with God on each one to do my best to follow the pattern of Philippians 4:6–7—to refuse to be anxious or worried, but in all things to pray with thanksgiving and experience God's peace.

It really isn't unpleasant situations or unpleasant people that upset us; it is the way we handle them that upsets us. For people who truly trust God, it doesn't matter if God removes the problem or gives them the strength to bear it. Either way, they put aside all anxiety and worry, and they remain at peace, because they know that God loves them and will always do what's best for them.

What Do You Think?

The thoughts we allow or disallow into our minds determine the measure of peace we either enjoy or forfeit. Isaiah addresses God in Isaiah 26:3, saying, "You keep him in perfect peace whose mind is stayed on you, because he trusts in you" (ESV).

Your thoughts determine your measure of peace.

We have the mind of Christ, according to 1 Corinthians 2:16. The amplification of this verse says that the mind of Christ refers to "the thoughts (feelings and purposes) of His heart" (AMPC). According to this scripture, we have the ability to think as Jesus would, but we must choose to do so.

Romans 8:6 says that we have the mind of the flesh and the mind of the Spirit, but once again, we choose the one from which we operate: "The mind governed by the flesh is death, but the mind governed by the Spirit is life and peace." If we choose to think according to the Spirit, we have life and peace. But if we choose to think according to the flesh, then we have death. According to the Amplified

Bible, Classic Edition, this "death" is "[death that comprises all the miseries arising from sin]." I would add that it also comprises the consequences of fleshly thinking. God has given us what we need to be able to think in ways that enable us to enjoy peace, but as always, He leaves the choice to us.

God has no interest in forcing us to do what is right, but He does want us to choose what is right. The way we think about the difficulties that arise in our lives determines how they affect us. If we think according to the flesh, our thoughts go something like this: *All I ever have are problems. I don't know why God allows these things to happen to me. Now I will have another miserable day. I'm worried about this situation, and I feel anxious because I don't know how to solve the problem.*

God wants you to choose to do what is right.

If we think according to the Spirit, our thoughts go something like this: *I wasn't expecting this problem, but I trust God to take care of me. I am going to pray about it and be thankful for all the blessings in my life. This problem is only one thing, and I have hundreds of things to be thankful for. God has always been faithful to me, and I know He won't let me down this time. This will work out for my good.* We can easily see how the fleshly thoughts make us miserable and how spiritual thoughts give us peace.

How do you normally think when you face problems, unexpected difficulties, or disappointments? Do you immediately worry and begin to feel anxious, or do you pray with thanksgiving and expect God to work something good out of the situation?

I think the most difficult trials to deal with are the ones that come unexpectedly, without warning. We may get up in the morning with wonderful plans for the day but suddenly have to deal with an unanticipated problem, and all our plans must change. These are difficult situations, but a correct response to them will allow us to still have a good day.

Casting Down Imaginations

Second Corinthians 10:4–5 (AMPC) says something that is important for all of us to understand:

> For the weapons of our warfare are not physical [weapons of flesh and blood], but they are mighty before God for the overthrow and destruction of strongholds, [inasmuch as we] refute arguments and theories and reasonings and every proud and lofty thing that sets itself up against the [true] knowledge of God; and we lead every thought and purpose away captive into the obedience of Christ (the Messiah, the Anointed One).

This passage teaches us that our spiritual weapons are effective "for the overthrow and destruction of strongholds" so we can "refute arguments and theories and reasonings and every proud and lofty thing" that comes against God and His Word. The King James Version of the Bible translates the second phrase as "casting down imaginations."

In order to fully understand this Scripture passage, please read it slowly, thinking about each point it makes:

- We are in a spiritual war.
- We have weapons.
- These weapons are mighty before God for the overthrow and destruction of strongholds.
- With these weapons, we refute arguments, theories, reasonings, and imaginations.
- We can lead every thought captive into the obedience of Jesus Christ.

Satan is your enemy, and he works to build strongholds in your mind.

A stronghold is an area occupied and dominated by an enemy. Satan is our enemy, and he works to build strongholds in our minds. We are to tear down these strongholds with God's Word by taking captive any thought that doesn't agree with His truth.

When I began my relationship with God through Christ, I had many strongholds in my mind because of my past life. The devil had lied to me for years, and I had thoughts such as *I will never overcome my past. I will always have a second-rate life because I was abused. Men cannot be trusted. I will take care of myself and never need anyone, because they would only let me down.*

Casting down these thoughts and replacing them with

God's promises took time and a lot of repetition, but now I am free, and I think totally differently than I did when I first became a Christian. The devil had told me the same lies over and over for years, and each time I refused a lie and replaced it with God's Word, the lie lost a little of its power. I kept it up, and I still practice declaring and meditating on God's Word.

When we have a problem, our imagination goes to work right away. We imagine (think) all kinds of awful things that may happen as a result of it. We imagine the problem will never go away. We imagine that it will get worse and we won't be able to deal with it. We imagine it will be more than we can take. We may begin to think that God doesn't love us or that we have done something wrong and conclude that this is why we have the problem. The misguided notions we can imagine and think about are endless, but we can defeat these mental strongholds if we will meditate on God's Word and let His truth replace the lies we have previously believed.

Satan's number one weapon against believers is deception. When we are deceived, we believe lies. Even though they are lies, they become realities to us if we believe them, and we cannot move past them until we learn the truth. God's Word is truth, and if we discipline ourselves to learn it and meditate on it regularly, it will renew our minds. Then, when we face unpleasant circumstances, we will enjoy the peace that passes understanding.

Satan's number one weapon is deception.

CHAPTER 10

Worry and Anxiety about Ourselves

An unpeaceful mind cannot operate normally. Hence the Apostle teaches us to "have no anxiety about anything" (Phil 4:6). Deliver all anxious thoughts to God as soon as they arise. Let the peace of God maintain your heart and mind (v. 7).

Watchman Nee[28]

Too many of us have the mistaken idea that God expects us to be perfect. If this were true, then He would not have needed to send Jesus to forgive our sins and to give us the Holy Spirit to help us in our weaknesses. When we put unreasonable expectations of perfection on ourselves, we fall short of reaching our goals and end up anxious and worried. We worry that we don't measure up, or that we are not good enough or not doing enough, that we don't look nice enough, are not intelligent enough, are not pleasing to God, and other things. These daily, seemingly small worries and anxieties can build and lead to a more serious situation, so we should learn how to cast each worry and care on the Lord, pray about our circumstances, be thankful for what we do right with God's help, and enjoy the peace that passes understanding.

Do not allow anxieties to pile up, but deal with each one as it comes.

It is never wise to let anxieties and worries pile up and become a heavy burden. Deal with each one as it comes, according to Philippians 4:6–7. If you do, the grace you need will be available for each day. Just as God gave the Israelites enough manna for one day, He also gives us grace for one day and expects us to trust Him for the next day.

It is wise to know how God sees you and feels about you, according to His Word. You are loved unconditionally by God, made right with Him through your faith in

Jesus, justified, sanctified, powerful, talented, creative, unique, and special—and you have many other wonderful qualities. If you know this, the enemy will not succeed in deceiving you.

You can and should take the pressure of trying to be perfect off yourself today by beginning to retrain your mind to know that you will not manifest perfection as long as you live in a flesh-and-blood body. The Garden of Eden was perfect, and Adam and Eve were perfect until they sinned. But since the fall of humanity, nothing in life has been perfect, and there are no perfect people. If you have an unrealistic expectation of yourself, other people, or your life, you will be disappointed.

God views us as perfect because of the work He has done in us through Christ, and even though we are continually growing toward manifesting more and more of that per-fection, we will not fully arrive until Jesus returns for us. We can have a perfect heart toward God and still not perform perfectly in everything we do. When Jesus returns to take us to heaven to live with Him for all eternity, we will be given a glorified body. Then we will be perfect, but not until then.

> *You can have a perfect heart toward God and still not perform perfectly.*

Matthew 5:48 says we should be perfect as our Father in heaven is perfect. When I first read this scripture, I felt I was trying to do something that I knew was impossible. The Amplified Bible, Classic Edition's rendering of it was very helpful to me: "You, therefore, must be perfect [growing into complete maturity of godliness in mind and character, having reached the proper height of virtue and integrity], as your heavenly Father is perfect." This taught me that being perfect means growing into complete maturity of mind and character and helped me to understand that positionally (in Christ) I was perfected, but experientially I was growing into it daily. We should always be growing spiritually, being gradually transformed into the image of

> You should always be growing spiritually.

Jesus Christ. The apostle Paul said that he was working toward that goal, and that although he had not attained it, he pressed on to make it his own:

> Not as though I had already attained, either were already perfect: but I follow after, if that I may apprehend that for which also I am apprehended of Christ Jesus. Brethren, I count not myself to have apprehended: but this one thing I do, forgetting those things which are behind, and reaching forth unto those things which are before, I press toward the mark for the prize of the high calling of God in Christ Jesus. ·
>
> Philippians 3:12–14 (KJV)

I want to behave perfectly, and if you love God, I'm sure you do too. The good news is that God looks at our heart (1 Samuel 16:7), and He sees us in Christ, who is perfect. This means that Christ's perfection is credited to us, just as our righteousness is credited to us because of our faith, according to Romans 4:23–24.

God Is Never Surprised

We want peace, and Jesus left us His peace, as we read in John 14:27; therefore, it is possible for us to have peace. But just as we should not be anxious and worried about our circumstances, neither should we be anxious and worried about our perfection, our past mistakes, or the mistakes we will make in the future.

> God knew everything you would do—right or wrong—and chose you anyway.

God knows everything all the time. He knew everything we would do—right or wrong—before we were ever born, and He chose us anyway. This is amazing, but true.

Jeremiah was a young man called by God to be a prophet, but he felt he was the wrong man for the job. See how God replied to Jeremiah's unbelief that God could use him:

> The word of the Lord came to me, saying, "Before I formed you in the womb I knew you, before you were born I set you apart; I appointed you as a prophet to the nations."
>
> "Alas, Sovereign Lord," I said, "I do not know how to speak; I am too young."
>
> But the Lord said to me, "Do not say, 'I am too young.' You must go to everyone I send you to and

say whatever I command you. Do not be afraid
of them, for I am with you and will rescue you,"
declares the Lord.

Jeremiah 1:4–8

Jeremiah didn't have a godly opinion of himself or his
abilities. God's Word does tell us not to think more highly
of ourselves than we ought to (Romans 12:3), but it never
tells us to have a poor opinion of ourselves. We should see
ourselves as "in Christ," and our confidence should be in
Him (Philippians 3:3). Our strengths and abilities are gifts
from Him, and our weaknesses should cause us to put our
trust in Him and joyfully watch Him work through us in
ways we could never imagine.

Jeremiah wasn't the first person to think he was the wrong
one to do something for God. When God called Moses to
deliver His people from bondage in Egypt, he protested and
then proceeded to tell God why he wasn't qualified (Exodus
3:7–4:17). Gideon did the same (Judges 6:11–23). God was
not pleased with these attitudes, but He was patient with
them and helped them grow into their calling.

Like Jeremiah, Moses, and Gideon, people usually focus on
their faults and fail to see their strengths, or they fail to realize that God's strength is made perfect in their weaknesses
(2 Corinthians 12:9). Psalm 139:13–14 teaches us that God created us in our mother's womb. God
does not make mistakes. You are
not a mistake, and you don't have to
worry about your imperfections.

You don't have to worry about your imperfections.

You may not like everything you do, but I urge you to embrace the wonderful and unique person God made you to be. Having a humble but good attitude about yourself is vital if you want to enjoy your life. You cannot be at peace with yourself if you are at war with yourself.

You may not see yourself as smart, strong, or something else you would like to be, but remember that God has "chosen the foolish things of the world to confound the wise" (1 Corinthians 1:27 KJV).

Our imperfections don't prevent God from using us. He is looking for availability, not ability. When God called me to teach His Word, I was a total mess. My soul was deeply wounded from the sexual abuse I had experienced during my childhood, and because of those wounds, my behavior was not good. My normal emotional state was angry, guilty, and fearful. I had one thing going for me, which was that I did love God. I didn't have a right relationship with Him, but I wanted to. God saw not only where I was but also where I would be if He gave me an opportunity and worked with me. The same is true for you.

As I studied God's Word to teach other people, I learned it myself. My mind was renewed, and as a result, I am a changed person now. I still have many imperfections, but I am always growing and have learned to be at peace with myself. I'm always making progress, and one year from now, I will be more advanced than I am now. You will be also if you continue to study and apply God's Word.

Being anxious about ourselves much of the time can

eventually cause deeper problems with anxiety, problems that may require professional help or medication to correct.

Some of Jesus' followers asked Him how they could please God, saying, "What must we do to do the works God requires?" (John 6:28). Jesus replied, "The work of God is this: to believe in the one he has sent" (John 6:29). If we would simply believe in God and obey His Word in every situation we encounter, we could eliminate anxiety and worry from our lives.

> Obey God's Word and you will eliminate anxiety from your life.

Believing God causes us to enter His supernatural rest (Hebrews 4:3), which is the peace that passes understanding.

Don't Look at Your Past

Isaiah instructs us regarding the importance of letting go of the past:

> Forget the former things; do not dwell on the past.
> See, I am doing a new thing! Now it springs up;
> do you not perceive it? I am making a way in the
> wilderness and streams in the wasteland.
>
> Isaiah 43:18–19

Pursue Peace

Before we can enjoy peace with ourselves, we must have peace with God. First Peter 3:10–11 (AMPC) taught me

Before you can enjoy peace, you must have peace with God.

the importance of being at peace with God, with myself, and with other people if I want to enjoy my life. This passage also taught me that if we want peace, we must search for it and "seek it eagerly," which is amplified to say, "[Do not merely desire peaceful relations with God, your fellowmen, and with yourself, but pursue, go after them!]"

At times in my life, I was praying for peace but not doing my part to obtain it. I was not pursuing peace and making it a major priority. I can tell you from experience that if

You have to pursue peace and seek it eagerly.

you want to enjoy a life of peace, you will have to pursue it, seek it eagerly, and be diligent in going after it. You will also need to be willing to make changes in the way you approach life. You may need to cut some things out of your schedule, slow down, or say no to things you know you should not do. You may need to identify your peace stealers, avoid them, and not allow Satan to take advantage of you through them. You may have to learn to not be touchy or easily offended, to forgive frequently and quickly, and to not worry and be anxious, but to take life as it comes, one day at a time. Peace is extremely valuable, and giving up anything that steals it from you is certainly worth doing.

To have peace with ourselves, we must first have peace with God. This comes in a personal relationship with Him through receiving Jesus as Lord and Savior and being obedient to Him as much as is possible. When you sin, as we all do, the way back to peace with God is to admit it, ask for God's forgiveness, receive His forgiveness, and then realize that your sin is in the past. Then you can do as Paul did: let go of what lies behind and press forward (Philippians 3:13).

When God forgives our sins, He forgets them and remembers them no more (Hebrews 10:17), and we should do the same. We must not carry a burden of guilt and condemnation for something that has been forgiven and is in the past. I believe that feeling guilty after we repent is our fleshly way of trying to pay for our sins. This is not right, because Jesus has already paid for them, and He doesn't need our help.

You can maintain peace with God through repenting for anything you believe you have done wrong. God already knows everything we will ever do wrong when He invites us into relationship with Him, and the forgiveness we need has already been provided through Jesus' death and resurrection. All we need to do is ask for and receive it.

Once we have peace with God, we can have peace with ourselves. More than forty years of experience in ministry has taught me that a large majority of people don't love themselves or have peace with themselves; therefore, they cannot love and have peace with the people in their lives. If this describes you, it is urgent for you to address the problem and see that God wants you to be at peace with yourself. The number of problems caused when we don't love ourselves in a balanced way is unimaginable.

Loving yourself is simply receiving the love of God. It isn't being in love with yourself or being self-centered; it is simply receiving by faith what God offers by His grace. His love is unconditional (has no conditions or strings attached), and therefore, we all meet the qualifications of receiving it. Just receive it and be thankful and amazed.

> Loving yourself is receiving by faith what God offers.

Reasons People Are Not at Peace with Themselves

One main reason many people are not at peace with themselves is that they let what others think and say about them determine how they feel about themselves. This is a serious mistake, because there will always be someone who has something unkind to think or say, and we must not let their opinions or words become our truth. Instead, we need to look at what God says about us and believe that. If we do, we will be at peace with ourselves.

> Embrace your uniqueness.

Another reason we may not be at peace with ourselves is that we compare ourselves to other people, thinking we should be like they are and do as they do. But God has created us all as unique people, and trying to be anyone other than who He has made us to be is not only exhausting but impossible. Ralph Waldo Emerson said, "To be yourself in a world that is constantly trying to make you something else is the greatest accomplishment."[29]

If you will embrace your uniqueness, you will be memorable. If you keep rejecting yourself and trying to be someone else, you will simply be frustrated.

We often exhaust ourselves trying to be something we can never be and were never intended to be because we want to be seen as perfect. Perfection this side of heaven is a myth. People torment themselves trying to achieve perfection so they

Perfection this side of heaven is a myth.

can feel good about themselves, but God never wants us to find our sense of self-worth in our own accomplishments. He wants us to know that our worth and value is in who we are in Christ and in our relationship with Him.

Some people cannot be at peace with themselves because they don't like the way they look or because of some other trait they have and wish they didn't. Others struggle because of traits they don't have and wish they did. For a long time, I didn't like my personality because I didn't feel I was like other women. I tried very hard to be what I thought was a "regular woman," one who made her family's clothes, grew a garden, canned vegetables, made jelly, was an expert at decorating her home, and awed her family daily with delicious meals.

But it just wasn't me! Any attempt I made to garden was a total failure. I could cook decently, but nothing fancy. And I did try to make Dave a pair of shorts after taking some sewing classes, but when I finished them, the pockets were longer than the shorts. Needless to say, they looked a bit strange.

I persecuted myself trying to be something that God had not created me to be. I was a good wife and a good mother, but I was also unique. I didn't do everything the same way other women did, and it took me several years of misery to finally realize that not being at peace with myself was hindering the entire plan God had for my life. It will do the same to yours if you are not at peace with yourself.

The way I felt about myself also made it impossible for me to have good relationships with other people. I frequently looked to them to give me what only God could give me: a sense of value.

Give yourself a big hug and say to yourself, "I accept you. I'm at peace with you, and I actually like you!" It could be the beginning of a great relationship.

I mentioned earlier in this book that while I was writing it, I was concerned about my upcoming cataract surgery. My eyes were very dry, and I had been told that surgery could make them worse. By the time I finished writing this book, the surgery was complete and I had had time to heal. I am very happy to report that my eyes are not drier than they were prior to the procedure—in fact, they are *less dry*! I had suffered so much with dry eyes before the operation that, to me, the fact that they are moister now is a miracle.

This simple little book can change your life if you will apply the principles that are in it. You don't have to be anxious and worried. God is offering you a better way, a peaceful way to live.

Any time anxious or worried thoughts enter your mind, remember Philippians 4:6–7. Determine to be anxious for nothing. Pray immediately; don't wait. Take action right away. Ask God to take care of the situation, and do it with a thankful heart for what He has already done in your life. As you do this, the peace that passes understanding will become yours. Remember that getting to this point is a process; you will have to be persistent and refuse to give up until peace is the normal condition in which you live.

Exodus 14:14 says, "The Lord will fight for you, *and you shall hold your peace* and remain at rest" (AMPC, emphasis added). The devil will definitely try to steal your peace, but you don't have to let him succeed. You can choose to hold on to it. When you feel your peace slipping away and anxiety rushing in, stand firm and remember that Jesus has given you His peace (John 14:27).

If you apply the lessons you have learned in this book a few times and feel that you are not getting any results, don't give up. That is what the devil wants you to do. Keep working at it, and each time you follow God's prescription for peace, you will make a little progress. The only people the devil can defeat are those who give up, and I don't believe you will do that. You are going to enjoy a new level of power because you are going to live in the peace that passes understanding. Remember, you don't need to have all of the answers to your problems because God does have them, and He is fighting for you.

1. "What Is Anxiety and Depression?" Anxiety and
   Depression Association of America, https://adaa.org
   /understanding-anxiety.
2. All of the following information and statistics are from
   "Did You Know?" Anxiety and Depression Association
   of America, https://adaa.org/understanding-anxiety
   /facts-statistics.
3. Corrie Ten Boom, *He Cares, He Comforts* (F. H. Revell,
   1977), 83.
4. Charles Stanley, "Victory over Anxiety," Facebook
   video, In Touch Ministries, March 11, 2021, https://
   www.facebook.com/watch/?v=815407555718497.
5. Quoted in Joseph Sutton, ed., *Words of Wellness: A
   Treasury of Quotations for Well-Being* (Hay House,
   1991).
6. Howard Taylor, *Hudson Taylor and the China Inland
   Mission* (Morgan and Scott, Ltd., 1920), 176.
7. Don Joseph Goewey, "85 Percent of What We Worry
   about Never Happens," *Huffington Post*, August 25,
   2015, https://www.huffpost.com/entry/85-of-what-we
   -worry-about_b_8028368.
8. Goewey, "85 Percent."
9. Charles Spurgeon, *The Salt-Cellars: Being a Collection
   of Proverbs, Together with Homely Notes* (A. C. Arm-
   strong, 1889), 62.
10. Quoted in Arthur T. Pierson, *The Miracles of Missions:
    Modern Marvels in the History of Missionary Enterprise*
    (Funk & Wagnalls, 1901), 197.

11. Rick Warren, *The Purpose of Christmas* (Simon & Schuster, 2012).

12. If you suffer with dry eye disease, you may be interested in knowing what I did. I will tell you, but I want to be clear that what I did may not be what you need at all. First, I went to my eye doctor again and asked if she could do anything to help me other than what she had already done. Instead of giving me one type of eyedrop for dry eyes, she gave me two types of drops and told me to layer them five minutes apart. Also, due to an eyelid surgery I had many years ago, my eyes don't close completely at night. Several people suggested wearing an eye mask, but masks didn't help until someone gave me one that is weighted with a material that feels similar to sand. That one helps a lot, and the weight on my eyes actually feels good.

13. Corrie Ten Boom, *Clippings from My Notebook* (Thomas Nelson, 1982), 21.

14. Quotefancy, https://quotefancy.com/quote/1557033 /Margaret-Cousins-Appreciation-can-make-a-day -even-change-a-life-Your-willingness-to-put.

15. BrainyQuote, https://www.brainyquote.com/quotes /william_arthur_ward_105516.

16. BrainyQuote, https://www.brainyquote.com/quotes /william_arthur_ward_105497.

17. Quotefancy, https://quotefancy.com/quote/2340252 /Hannah-Whitall-Smith-The-soul-that-gives-thanks -can-find-comfort-in-everything-the-soul.

18. Dietrich Bonhoeffer, *Life Together: The Classic Exploration of Faith in Community* (Harper & Row, 1954), 29.

19. "10 Billy Graham Quotes on Thankfulness," Billy Graham Evangelistic Association, November 14, 2019, https://billygraham.org/story/billy-graham-quotes-thankfulness/.

20. Khalil Gibran, *The Kahlil Gibran Reader: Inspirational Writings* (Kensington Publishing Corporatation, 2006), 45.

21. Marc Chernoff, "18 Great Reminders When You're Having a Bad Day," *Marc and Angel Hack Life* (blog), October 19, 2014, https://www.marcandangel.com/2014/10/19/18-great-reminders-when-youre-having-a-bad-day.

22. "10 Unforgettable Quotes by Jim Rohn," JimRohn.com, September 13, 2019, https://www.jimrohn.com/10-unforgettable-quotes-by-jim-rohn.

23. "The Choice of Gratitude," Henri Nouwen Society, July 2, 2021, https://henrinouwen.org/meditations/the-choice-of-gratitude.

24. AZ Quotes, https://www.azquotes.com/quote/725971.

25. Quoted in George Sweeting, *Who Said That? More Than 2,500 Usable Quotes and Illustrations* (Moody Publishers, 1995).

26. "The Real Meaning of Peace," All Time Short Stories, May 7, 2016, https://alltimeshortstories.com/meaning-of-peace.

27. AZ Quotes, https://www.azquotes.com/author/12905-Saint_Francis_de_Sales.

28. Jack Wellman, "24 Quotes about Anxiety," ChristianQuotes.info, December 8, 2015, https://www.christianquotes.info/quotes-by-topic/quotes-about-anxiety.

29. BrainyQuote, https://www.brainyquote.com/quotes/ralph_waldo_emerson_387459.

Do you have a real relationship with Jesus?

God loves you! He created you to be a special, unique, one-of-a-kind individual, and He has a specific purpose and plan for your life. And through a personal relationship with your Creator—God—you can discover a way of life that will truly satisfy your soul.

No matter who you are, what you've done, or where you are in your life right now, God's love and grace are greater than your sin—your mistakes. Jesus willingly gave His life so you can receive forgiveness from God and have new life in Him. He's just waiting for you to invite Him to be your Savior and Lord.

If you are ready to commit your life to Jesus and follow Him, all you have to do is ask Him to forgive your sins and give you a fresh start in the life you are meant to live. Begin by praying this prayer...

Lord Jesus, thank You for giving Your life for me and forgiving me of my sins so I can have a personal relationship with You. I am sincerely sorry for the mistakes I've made, and I know I need You to help me live right.

Your Word says in Romans 10:9, "If you declare with your mouth, 'Jesus is Lord,' and believe in your heart that God raised him from the dead, you will be saved" (NIV). I believe You are the Son of God and confess You as my Savior and Lord. Take me just as I am, and work in my heart, making me the person You want me to be. I want to live for You, Jesus, and I am so grateful that You are giving me a fresh start in my new life with You today.

I love You, Jesus!

It's so amazing to know that God loves us so much! He wants to have a deep, intimate relationship with us that grows every day as we spend time with Him in prayer and Bible study. And we want to encourage you in your new life in Christ.

Please visit joycemeyer.org/salvation to request Joyce's book *A New Way of Living*, which is our gift to you. We also have other free resources online to help you make progress in pursuing everything God has for you.

Congratulations on your fresh start in your life in Christ! We hope to hear from you soon.

Joyce Meyer is one of the world's leading practical Bible teachers. A *New York Times* bestselling author, Joyce's books have helped millions of people find hope and restoration through Jesus Christ. Joyce's program, *Enjoying Everyday Life*, is broadcast on television, radio, and online to millions worldwide in over 100 languages.

Through Joyce Meyer Ministries, Joyce teaches internationally on a number of topics with a particular focus on how the Word of God applies to our everyday lives. Her candid communication style allows her to share openly and practically about her experiences so others can apply what she has learned to their lives.

Joyce has authored more than 140 books, which have been translated into more than 160 languages, and over 39 million of her books have been distributed worldwide. Bestsellers include *Power Thoughts*; *The Confident Woman*; *Look Great, Feel Great*; *Starting Your Day Right*; *Ending Your Day Right*; *Approval Addiction*; *How to Hear from God*; *Beauty for Ashes*; and *Battlefield of the Mind*.

Joyce's passion to help hurting people is foundational to the vision of Hand of Hope, the missions arm of Joyce

Meyer Ministries. Each year Hand of Hope provides millions of meals for the hungry and malnourished, installs freshwater wells in poor and remote areas, provides critical relief after natural disasters, and offers free medical and dental care to thousands through their hospitals and clinics worldwide. Through Project GRL, women and children are rescued from human trafficking and provided safe places to receive an education, nutritious meals, and the love of God.

US & FOREIGN OFFICE
ADDRESSES

Joyce Meyer Ministries
P.O. Box 655
Fenton, MO 63026
USA
(636) 349-0303

Joyce Meyer Ministries—Canada
P.O. Box 7700
Vancouver, BC V6B 4E2
Canada
(800) 868-1002

Joyce Meyer Ministries—Australia
Locked Bag 77
Mansfield Delivery Centre
Queensland 4122
Australia
(07) 3349 1200

Joyce Meyer Ministries—England
P.O. Box 1549
Windsor SL4 1GT
United Kingdom
01753 831102

Joyce Meyer Ministries—South Africa
P.O. Box 5
Cape Town 8000
South Africa
(27) 21-701-1056

Joyce Meyer Ministries—Francophonie
29 avenue Maurice Chevalier
77330 Ozoir la Ferriere
France

Joyce Meyer Ministries—Germany
Postfach 761001
22060 Hamburg
Germany
+49 (0)40 / 88 88 4 11 11

Joyce Meyer Ministries—Netherlands
Lorenzlaan 14
7002 HB Doetinchem
+31 657 555 9789

Joyce Meyer Ministries—Russia
P.O. Box 789
Moscow 101000
Russia
+7 (495) 727-14-68

100 Inspirational Quotes
100 Ways to Simplify Your Life
21 Ways to Finding Peace and Happiness
Any Minute
Approval Addiction
The Approval Fix
Authentically, Uniquely You*
The Battle Belongs to the Lord
Battlefield of the Mind*
Battlefield of the Mind Bible
Battlefield of the Mind for Kids
Battlefield of the Mind for Teens
Battlefield of the Mind Devotional
Battlefield of the Mind New Testament
Be Anxious for Nothing*
Being the Person God Made You to Be
Beauty for Ashes
Change Your Words, Change Your Life
Colossians: A Biblical Study
The Confident Mom
The Confident Woman
The Confident Woman Devotional
Do It Afraid*
Do Yourself a Favor...Forgive
Eat the Cookie...Buy the Shoes
Eight Ways to Keep the Devil under Your Feet
Ending Your Day Right
Enjoying Where You Are on the Way to Where You Are Going
Ephesians: A Biblical Study
The Everyday Life Bible
The Everyday Life Psalms and Proverbs
Filled with the Spirit
Galatians: A Biblical Study
Good Health, Good Life
Habits of a Godly Woman
Healing the Soul of a Woman*
Healing the Soul of a Woman Devotional
Hearing from God Each Morning
How to Age without Getting Old
How to Hear from God*

Start Your New Life Today
Starting Your Day Right
Straight Talk
Teenagers Are People Too!
Trusting God Day by Day
The Word, the Name, the Blood
Woman to Woman
You Can Begin Again
Your Battles Belong to the Lord*

JOYCE MEYER SPANISH TITLES

Auténtica y única (Authentically, Uniquely You)
Belleza en lugar de cenizas (Beauty for Ashes)
Buena salud, buena vida (Good Health, Good Life)
Cambia tus palabras, cambia tu vida (Change Your Words, Change Your Life)
El campo de batalla de la mente (Battlefield of the Mind)
Cómo envejecer sin avejentarse (How to Age without Getting Old)
Como formar buenos habitos y romper malos habitos (Making Good Habits, Breaking Bad Habits)
La conexión de la mente (The Mind Connection)
Dios no está enojado contigo (God Is Not Mad at You)
La dosis de aprobación (The Approval Fix)
Efesios: Comentario biblico (Ephesians: Biblical Commentary)
Empezando tu día bien (Starting Your Day Right)
Hágalo con miedo (Do It Afraid)
Hazte un favor a ti mismo...perdona (Do Yourself a Favor...Forgive)
Madre segura de sí misma (The Confident Mom)
Momentos de quietud con Dios (Quiet Times with God Devotional)
Mujer segura de sí misma (The Confident Woman)
No se afane por nada (Be Anxious for Nothing)
Pensamientos de poder (Power Thoughts)
Sanidad para el alma de una mujer (Healing the Soul of a Woman)
Sanidad para el alma de una mujer, devocionario (Healing the Soul of a Woman Devotional)
Santiago: Comentario bíblico (James: Biblical Commentary)
Sobrecarga (Overload)*
Sus batallas son del Señor (Your Battles Belong to the Lord)
Termina bien tu día (Ending Your Day Right)
Tienes que atreverte (I Dare You)
Usted puede comenzar de nuevo (You Can Begin Again)

Viva amando su vida (Living a Life You Love)
Viva valientemente (Living Courageously)
Vive por encima de tus sentimientos (Living beyond Your Feelings)

* Study Guide available for this title

BOOKS BY DAVE MEYER

Life Lines